As we live our lives, we repeatedly make decisions that shape our future circumstances and affect the sort of person we will be. When choosing whether to start a family, or deciding on a career, we often think we can assess the options by imagining what different experiences would be like for us. L. A. Paul argues that, for choices involving dramatically new experiences, we are confronted by the brute fact that we can know very little about our subjective futures. This has serious implications for our decisions. If we make life choices in the way we naturally and intuitively want to—by considering what we care about, and what our future selves will be like if we choose to have the experience—we only learn what we really need to know after we have already committed ourselves. If we try to escape the dilemma by avoiding an experience, we have still made a choice.

Choosing rationally, then, may require us to regard big life decisions as choices to make discoveries, small and large, about the intrinsic nature of experience, and to recognize that part of the value of living authentically is to experience one's life and preferences in whatever way they may evolve in the wake of the choices one makes.

Using classic philosophical examples about the nature of consciousness, and drawing on recent work in normative decision theory, cognitive science, epistemology, and the philosophy of mind, Paul develops a rigorous account of transformative experience that sheds light on how we should understand real-world experience and our capacity to rationally map our subjective futures.

L. A. PAUL

# TRANSFORMATIVE
# EXPERIENCE

OXFORD
UNIVERSITY PRESS

# OXFORD
### UNIVERSITY PRESS

Great Clarendon Street, Oxford, OX2 6DP,
United Kingdom

Oxford University Press is a department of the University of Oxford.
It furthers the University's objective of excellence in research, scholarship,
and education by publishing worldwide. Oxford is a registered trade mark of
Oxford University Press in the UK and in certain other countries

Published in the United States of America by Oxford University Press
198 Madison Avenue, New York, NY 10016, United States of America

British Library Cataloguing in Publication Data
Data available

Library of Congress Cataloging in Publication Data
Data available

ISBN 978–0–19–871795–9 (Hbk.)
ISBN 978–0–19–877731–1 (Pbk.)

*For Kieran*

# ACKNOWLEDGEMENTS

I am very grateful for comments and discussion from Marilyn Adams, Robert Adams, Marcus Arvan, Elizabeth Barnes, Tim Bayne, Helen Beebee, Gordon Belot, Teresa Blankmeyer Burke, Rachael Briggs, Sarah Broadie, Lara Buchak, John Campbell, Herman Cappelen, David Chalmers, Ruth Chang, John Collins, Philip A. Cowan, Kenny Easwaran, Andy Egan, Jordan S. Ellenberg, Owain Evans, Branden Fitelson, Hannah Ginsborg, Philip Goff, Alison Gopnik, Tom Griffiths, Jennifer Groh, Alan Hájek, Joe Halpern, Kieran Healy, Jenann Ismael, Jack Knight, Matt Kotzen, Jonathan Livengood, Tania Lombrozo, Bill Lycan, John MacFarlane, Rachael V. McKinnon, Christia Mercer, Peter Momtchiloff, Richard Moran, Sarah Moss, Ram Neta, John Quiggin, Carla Merino Rajme, Geoffrey Sayre-McCord, Jonathan Schaffer, Tamar Schapiro, Eric Schliesser, Laura Schulz, David Sobel, Cynthia Stark, Sharon Street, Michael Strevens, Meghan Sullivan, Justin Systma, Josh Tenenbaum, Jason Turner, Paul Weirich, Caroline West, and J. R. G. Williams.

Special thanks are due to Tyler Doggett for several illuminating conversations, and to Richard Pettigrew, Rachael Briggs, and Neil Levy for reading the entire manuscript and giving me extensive comments. Research for the book was partly supported by a Fellowship with the National Humanities Center and by a John Simon Guggenheim Memorial Foundation Fellowship.

I am especially indebted to Kieran Healy, who spent endless hours patiently debating these ideas with me, and made many suggestions that, when I had the sense to adopt them, greatly improved the book.

# CONTENTS

"And if Eeyore's back snapped suddenly, then we could all laugh. Ha ha! Amusing in a quiet way," said Eeyore, "but not really helpful."

"Well," said Piglet meekly, "I thought—"

"Would it break your back, Eeyore?" asked Pooh, very much surprised.

"That's what would be so interesting, Pooh. Not being quite sure till afterwards."

Pooh said "Oh!" and they all began to think again.

A. A. Milne, *Winnie the Pooh*

# CHAPTER 1

# BECOMING A VAMPIRE

Imagine that you have the chance to become a vampire. With one swift, painless bite, you'll be permanently transformed into an elegant and fabulous creature of the night. As a member of the undead, your life will be completely different. You'll experience a range of intense, revelatory new sense experiences, you'll gain immortal strength, speed and power, and you'll look fantastic in everything you wear. You'll also need to drink blood and avoid sunlight.

Suppose that all of your friends, people whose interests, views and lives were similar to yours, have already decided to become vampires. And all of them tell you that they *love* it. They describe their new lives with unbridled enthusiasm, and encourage you to become a vampire too. They assuage your fears and explain that modern vampires don't kill humans; they drink the blood of cows and chickens. They say things like: "I'd never go back, even if I could. Life has meaning and a sense of purpose now that it never had when I was human. I understand Reality in a way I just couldn't before. It's amazing. But I can't really explain it to you, a mere human—you have to be a vampire to know what it's like."[1] Suppose that you also know that if you pass up this opportunity up, you'll never have another chance.

## Would You Do It?

To make a choice like this, you'd want to make the best decision you could. And that means you'd want to proceed as rationally as possible.

---

[1] I thank Jordan S. Ellenberg for suggesting I use vampires to illustrate my thesis. See Ellenberg (2013).

Becoming a vampire would be big—really big. It obviously isn't a decision to be undertaken lightly. You'd want to choose the smartest option, the option that would make your life as good as it could be after you'd made your choice. You wouldn't want to pass up one of the most amazing experiences you could ever have. But you wouldn't want to make a huge mistake either.

The trouble is, in this situation, *how could you possibly make an informed choice?* For, after all, you cannot know what it is like to be a vampire until you are one. And if you can't know what it's like to be a vampire without becoming one, you can't compare the character of the lived experience of what it is like to be you, right now, a mere human, to the character of the lived experience of what it would be like to be a vampire. This means that, if you want to make this choice by considering what you want your lived experience to be like in the future, you can't do it rationally. At least, you can't do it by weighing the competing options concerning what it would be like and choosing on this basis. And it seems awfully suspect to rely solely on the testimony of your vampire friends to make your choice, because, after all, they aren't human any more, so their preferences are the ones vampires have, not the ones humans have.

This book argues that we find ourselves in this sort of situation for some of our most significant life decisions. In other words, in the real world, as we face our own personal series of life choices, some of these choices are, in a very important sense, like the choice to become a vampire. While life choices don't usually involve the possibility of becoming an immortal being, they are fundamentally similar in a different way.

The idea is that, when you find yourself facing a decision involving a new experience that is unlike any other experience you've had before, you can find yourself in a special sort of epistemic situation. In this sort of situation, you know very little about your possible future, in the same way that you are limited when you face a possible future as a vampire. And so, if you want to make the decision by thinking about what your lived experience would be like if you decided to undergo the experience, you have a problem.

In such a situation, you find yourself facing a decision where you lack the information you need to make the decision the way you naturally want to make it—by assessing what the different possibilities would be like and choosing between them. The problem is pressing, because many of life's big personal decisions are like this: they involve the choice to undergo a dramatically new experience that will change your life in important ways, and an essential part of your deliberation concerns what your future life will be like if you decide to undergo the change. But as it turns out, like the choice to become a vampire, many of these big decisions involve choices to have experiences that teach us things we cannot know about from any other source but the experience itself.

When we face a choice like this, we can't know what our lives will be like until we've undergone the new experience, but if we don't undergo the experience, we won't know what we are missing. And, further, many of these new and unknown experiences are life-changing or dramatically personally transformative. So not only must you make the choice without knowing what it will be like if you choose to have the new experience, but the choice is big, and you know it is big. You know that undergoing the experience will change what it is like for you to live your life, and perhaps even change what it is like to *be* you, deeply and fundamentally.

I will not argue that you can't get information from the testimony of others when you make such choices. You can. But I will argue that such guidance only goes so far, for the information such sources can supply is incomplete. So while we should consider the information we can gather from science and from the advice of friends and relatives, in the end, we must decide for ourselves, weighing incomplete evidence in the light of our own personal preferences.

I will not argue that you can't change the way you make the decision. You can. You could change the way you decide, such that the new deliberation does not rely on your expectations about what it would be like for *you* to have the experience, or does not involve weighing advice and testimony from your own personal perspective and deciding how much of it applies to you personally, but rather, relies solely on impersonal facts about how people, in general, respond to these kinds of experiences. In other words, you can replace your personal approach to decision-making with impersonal decision-making, removing any crucial role for your experience or your individual, personal perspective when you deliberate.

But changing the decision this way gives an unsatisfying answer to the question of how you should make these deeply personal, centrally important, life-changing decisions. For after all, your decision concerns *your* personal future, and so an essential part of your decision is based on what it would be like for *you* to have the experience and to live the life you bring about for yourself. You naturally and intuitively want to make your life choices by thinking about what you care about and what your future experience will be like if you decide to undergo the experience. This is why you are expected to weigh evidence from your own personal perspective and decide how you want to apply it to your own situation. Making the decision into one where what it would be like for you is no longer a consideration, is not a decision you care about in the same way.

So, in many ways, large and small, as we live our lives, we find ourselves confronted with a brute fact about how little we can know about our futures, just when it is most important to us that we do know. For many big life choices, we only learn what we need to know after we've done it, and we change ourselves in the process of doing it. I'll argue that, in the end, the best response to this situation is to choose based on whether we want to discover who we'll become.[2]

---

[2] In the Afterword, I'll explore connections to empirical and theoretical issues in economics, statistics, and psychology, and will consider ways to develop new models for rational decision-making in contexts of transformative choice.

CHAPTER 2

# TRANSFORMATIVE CHOICE

There are conscious animals whose experiences are very unlike our own. Animals whose sensory apparatus is similar to ours, like dogs, see things with their eyes and hear things with their ears. But dogs can hear sounds and smell smells that humans can't, and their overall experience of the world around them is rich with sensory information that humans either can't or don't notice. What it is like to be a dog is very different from what it is like to be a human.

Animals with radically different sensory equipment from ours have dramatically different experiences from us. An octopus experiences much of the world through its arms, which have independent abilities to sense and respond to stimuli. The octopus's arms may even have an independent ability to think for themselves, since the arms seem to act independently from the rest of the octopus under certain conditions. What is it like to have arms that can act and think for themselves? While we can come up with creative vignettes that may capture some of the functional features of this arrangement, we should not imagine that we know what it is like to be such a creature.[1]

Another example, drawn from a claim famously defended by Thomas Nagel, is the experience of the bat.[2] As Nagel points out,

---

[1] Peter Godfrey Smith (2013), rather surprisingly, claims that we can know what it is like by knowing enough to be able to predict what the octopus is likely to do. I don't think this captures knowledge of what it is like to be an octopus, no more than I can know what it is like to be a spider (or a vampire!) simply because I know it is likely to drink the blood of its prey.

[2] Nagel (1974) and Nagel (1989) uses the example of what it's like for a cockroach to taste scrambled eggs.

the bat "sees" via echolocation, emitting sound waves that are bounced off of objects in the environment and, when experienced, allow the bat to detect insects and other tasty dinner options. Dolphins also echolocate, and even humans do, for example, when we hear footsteps coming down a corridor. What is it like to be an echolocating bat? What is it like to have the conscious experience or perspective of an animal who can "see" in the dark in this way? Again, while we can imagine being in the dark, hearing noises that we use to judge positions of objects, and finding certain insects tasty, we nevertheless cannot know what it is like to be a bat, which is an animal whose perspective, as Nagel puts it, is "fundamentally *alien*" to us.

There are examples closer to home. Imagine that neuroscientists and engineers invent a microchip that, when implanted in the brain, gives humans a new sensory ability, a sixth sense in addition to the usual five. If this sense is truly new, rather than a combination of more familiar senses, before getting the chip, we cannot know what it would be like to experience the new, sixth, sense. With respect to this sensory ability, anyone without the chip would be in the same position as a person who is blind from birth, or a person who has never been able to hear: there would be a human sensory ability that some people have and others don't, but those without the chip would not know what it is like to have it until they experience it. The same applies to other experiences; if you have never seen color, you cannot know what it is like to see lime green. If you have never heard sound, you cannot know what it is like to hear *St. John's Passion*.

Another way to grasp the idea is to take a historical perspective, and think of trying to explain modern life to a person from 400 BC. Such a person could not know what it is like to use a computer or to fly in a plane. Similar points apply to the distant future, with all its impending marvels. We can tell interesting stories, but if the world changes as much as it has over the past 2,500 years, knowing what it would be like to live 2,500 years from now is beyond our capacities.

In fact, humans vary so much and so deeply, that even small differences (contextually speaking) in experiences between people can prevent us from knowing what it is like to be a different type of person. People who are not from wealthy, Western societies can interpret and experience the world in radically different ways from people who are. People with different skin colors, genders, or histories will have very different experiences in their day-to-day interactions. If you are a man who has grown up and always lived in a rich Western country, you cannot know what it is like to be an impoverished woman living in Ethiopia, and if she has never left her village, she cannot know what it is like be a man like you. If you are a white businessman living in San Francisco in 2013 you cannot know what it was like to be a black man involved in the Jamaican rebellion in 1760, hiding out in the forest in the dead of night while British troops comb the island trying to hunt you down,[3] or know what it was like to be a slave in the American South.[4] "I took the opportunity to investigate this abominable sistem of slavery...I have examend their instruments of torture the stocks whip and paddle and strap...Solomans book [Solomon Northrup's *Twelve Years a Slave*] is true to the letter only it dos not portray the system as bad as it is it is not in the power of man to do it."[5] There are many other potential points of difference: for example, if you have always been happy with the gender identity assigned to you at birth, you cannot know what it is like to be forced to live with a gender identity you reject.

---

[3] Brown (2003).

[4] We might know *something* about how different the experience would be if we have some first person narratives of related experiences. John Howard Griffin's (1961) *Black Like Me* is a classic piece of testimony about how a temporary change in skin color can lead to radically new experiences. But dyeing our skin or reading stories still won't teach us what it is really like. It's a difficult question to figure out what it *does* teach us. See Paul (1997) for related discussion.

[5] Entry from the diary of John Burrud, Union soldier, May 21, 1863, quoted by Alan Rothman (2014) in "The horrors '12 Years a Slave' couldn't tell."

All of these examples bring out the deep and familiar fact that different subjective points of view, as different conscious perspectives, can be fundamentally inaccessible to each other. Unless you've had the relevant experiences, what it is like to be a person or an animal very different from yourself is, in a certain fundamental way, inaccessible to you. It isn't that you can't imagine something in place of the experience you haven't had. It's that this act of imagining isn't enough to let you know what it is *really* like to be an octopus, or to be a slave, or to be blind. You need to have the experience itself to know what it is really like.

This brings out another, somewhat less familiar fact about the relationship between knowledge and experience: just as knowledge about the experience of one individual can be inaccessible to another individual, what you can know about yourself at one time can be inaccessible to you at another time. For example, you can have an experience that is so unlike previous experiences you've had, that before you have the new experience, you cannot know what it is going to be like for you to have it.

## Experience Is the Best Teacher

Frank Jackson exploits the fact that what you can know about yourself at one time can be inaccessible to you at another time in a famous thought experiment about Mary, who, from birth, has lived in a black-and-white room.[6] When Mary finally decides to leave her room, she sees color for the first time. We can tell the story so that, following Jackson, her first color experience is of something red. When Mary sees red, she has a dramatically new experience: she now knows what it is like to see red, and more generally, she now knows what it is like to see color. But before she left her room, Mary could not have known what this would be like. All the imagining she could do would not be enough for her to

---

[6] Jackson (1982).

know what it was like to see color. Her first experience of seeing color was so unlike any experience she'd ever had before she left her room that she could not have known what it was going to be like to see red.

Jackson's example is designed to support the claim that, even if Mary was some kind of super-scientist who knew all that science could ever tell us about the science of color experience, she still couldn't know what it was like to see red until she left her room. But we don't need an example that's this far-fetched, for we are not concerned with defending Jackson's conclusion. Our interest is in decisions about new experiences that we need to make under ordinary circumstances, when we aren't super-scientists and we are simply relying on the best science available.[7]

Our version of the example will concern ordinary Mary, who we may assume knows only what contemporary science can tell her about color experience, and has friends on the outside who describe to her, as best they can, what it's like to see red. As she decides whether to leave her room, Mary reads stories about what it is like to see red, consults textbooks, and has friends tell her about their experience of what it is like. Before leaving her room, she might imagine undergoing some sort of experience that is surprising and intense and emotional. But these descriptions, stories, and testimony won't teach her what it will be like to see color for the first time. Ordinary Mary does not and could not know what it is like to see color, and so she cannot know

---

[7] Since I am just concerned here with experience in ordinary circumstances, I am not taking a stand on physicalism, or whether there is such a thing as phenomenal consciousness or a way it is like from a first person perspective that couldn't, in principle, be completely cashed out in terms of third person facts. I take it that contemporary science is incomplete with regard to its account of first personal experience, and so decision-makers in the real world are like ordinary Mary rather than Jackson's Mary. Even if super-scientist Mary would only gain a new ability of some sort when she saw red for the first time, ordinary Mary would gain new knowledge. (And in any case, the new ability is necessary for the sort of rational evaluation being considered.)

what it will be like for her to see color until she's left her room.[8] In other words, ordinary Mary, before she leaves her room, is in a special kind of epistemic poverty, keyed to her inability to grasp crucial information about the nature of her future experiences.[9]

Once Mary leaves her room, her experience transforms her epistemic perspective, and by doing so, it transforms her point of view. When she sees color for the first time, she gains new knowledge by having this experience: she gains knowledge about what something is like, namely, what it is like for her to see color, and by extension, how she'll react to that experience. And once she has this knowledge, she is able to imagine and envision what it is like to see color, and to model her responses. David Lewis puts it beautifully: "What's essential is that when we learn what an experience is like by having it, we gain abilities to remember, imagine and recognize."[10]

This type of knowledge or ability requires experience. For Mary to be able to successfully project forward into her subjective future and imaginatively represent what it's like for her to experience color, she needs the relevant sort of prior experience. "There's truth to this. If you want to know what some new and different experience is like, you can learn it by going out and really *having* that experience. You can't learn it by being told about the experience, however thorough your lessons may be" (Lewis 1988, p. 29).

When a person has a new and different kind of experience, a kind of experience that teaches her something she could not have learned without having that kind of experience, she has an *epistemic transformation*. Her knowledge of what something is like, and thus

---

[8] Again, my claim that she could not have known what it was like is indexed to her ordinary circumstances. Given our current best science, and given her experiences up to that point, Mary could not know what it would be like to see color.

[9] I am making no assumption here that the new information ordinary Mary grasps isn't physical information.

[10] Lewis (1988). Some argue that when Mary learns what it is like to see red, she does so by grasping a phenomenal concept. See, e.g., Goff (2011) for discussion and criticism.

her subjective point of view, changes. With this new experience, she gains new abilities to cognitively entertain certain contents, she learns to understand things in a new way, and she may even gain new information. For any epistemic transformation, the degree of epistemic change depends on how much the person already knows, and on the type of experience that is involved.[11]

Perhaps because we value gains in cognitive abilities, understanding, and information, what it's like to have experiences matters to us. Our experiences, especially new ones, are valuable, that is, we value having them, and we especially care about having experiences of different sorts.[12] As such, experiences have values that carry weight in our decision-making.[13] Such values are first personal, psychological values, and can be described as the values of what it is like to have the experiences or of what it is like to be in these experiential states. (I will assume that an experience has this sort of value only when it correctly represents what's in the world or it is produced in the right way. So these

---

[11] If we fine grain experiences, such that just about any experience can count as "new and different," then many experiences can count as epistemically transformative, but will usually be so in uninteresting ways. For example, perhaps the cup of coffee I'm about to drink is very slightly unlike any other cup of coffee I've ever had, because it is slightly more acidic in flavor. Obviously, this fact is rather uninteresting. It is more natural, especially in a decision-theoretic context, to partition new experiences in a coarse-grained way, perhaps into natural experiential kinds. On such a partition, epistemically transformative experiences involve experiences of new and different, reasonably natural experiential kinds. While the types of epistemically transformative experiences I focus on in this book are clearly transformative, in other cases, the relevant change might be a matter of degree.

[12] These values are not first-order values of happiness or unhappiness or "hedons," they are intrinsic first-order values tied to the character of the experience itself. My view of the intrinsic value relates to Thomas Nagel's question about why death can be bad for the deceased, for the person who dies can no longer enjoy the intrinsic value of having experiences. (I thank Tyler Doggett for discussion here.)

[13] In his (1989) "Dispositional theories of value," David Lewis defends the assignment of value to something in terms of valuing it in ideal circumstances of full imaginative acquaintance.

values are values for lived experience, where such experience is "real" or veridical.)[14]

I take these values of experiences to be values that do not reduce to anything else: they are primitive and they are not merely values of pleasure and pain. Instead, the values are widely variable, intrinsic, complex, and grounded by the nature of experience.[15] Such values, as I shall understand them, are values that can be grounded by more than merely qualitative or sensory characters, as they may also arise nonsensory features of experiences, especially rich, developed experiences that embed a range of mental states, including beliefs, emotions, and desires.

These values can be had by a range of diverse experiences, such as what it is like to make a new discovery or what it is like to suffer from the loss of a loved one. Because I take such values to extend past the merely qualitative, and to capture the rich, complex nature of lived experiences resulting from our sensory as well as our nonsensory cognitive phenomenology, I will describe them as *subjective values*.[16] A subjective value need not be determined solely by the experience's cognitive phenomenological character. But even in that case, the subjective value is discovered or made cognitively accessible by the discovery

[14] I don't, in fact, think correct representation or veridicality is necessary for an experience to have this sort of subjective value (although it might affect how valuable the experience is or the quality of value it has), but arguing the point here will take me too far afield.

[15] I am not assuming that these intrinsic values are incomparable or incommensurable. For more on incomparability and incommensurability, see Chang (1997). For developed discussion of the experiential grounds for subjective value, see Paul (2015b), section 6.3, pp. 513–17. In this book, I will sometimes discuss experience in terms of 'cognitive phenomenology', though endorsing the notion of cognitive phenomenology isn't required for my arguments to go through. For developed discussions of cognitive phenomenology, see Tim Bayne and Michelle Montague (2011); and Horgan and Tienson (2002) for a seminal defense of the importance of the connection between phenomenology and conscious cognitive states.

[16] We could tie them to the contents of our experience, if those contents are rich enough. We could certainly include the contents of experience in the ground for the subjective value. See Siegel (2012) *The Contents of Visual Experience*.

of the phenomenological character. In Lewisian terms, we might say that, by having the experience, we gain the ability to assess the subjective value of the experience by gaining the ability to grasp it using our first-personal, imaginative perspective. (The subjective value of a lived experience whose value is partly derived from nonphenomenological features may be inaccessible until one has the requisite experience needed for the individual to be able to grasp its subjective value, that is, the experience is needed to give us access to the subjective value, even if the value is grounded on more than mere phenomenology.) Subjective values, grounded by what it is like to have lived experiences, are first-personal values that can range from the value of hearing beautiful music, to the value of tasting a ripe peach, to the value of adopting a new sense of self as a consequence of a major life event.

Take Mary's experience of seeing color for the first time. Having that experience has an intrinsic subjective value for her, a value grounded by what it is like for her to see color for the first time. This is an overall subjective value that includes the purely qualitative value of what it is like to see red along with what it is like for her to have this possibly thrilling, or perhaps frightening, new experience. Having the experience for the first time involves a kind of revelation: when she sees red for the first time, the intrinsic nature of having that visual experience is revealed to her, and only once she knows this intrinsic nature can she assign the experience a subjective value.[17] Subsequent experiences she has, such as experiences that are enriched in various ways by the new information she has acquired, also have subjective values.

What we learn from the case of Mary is that stories, testimony, and theories aren't enough to teach you what it is like to have truly new types of experiences—you learn what it is like by actually having an experience of that type. Unless and until scientists discover how we are to leap the explanatory gap between scientific theory and experience, real people face this kind of epistemic limitation, that is, real people (including

---

[17] Here I am using Campbell's (1993) notion of revelation for my own ends. Also see Johnston (1992)'s discussion of revelation in "How to speak of the colors."

scientists) can't know what it is like to have new experiences just from knowing what scientists know right now about how the brain works. Given this, you must have had the right kind of experience to know a subjective value, because you must know what an experience of that type is like to know its value—for example, you must experience color before you can know the subjective value of what it's like to see color.[18]

Of course, to have an epistemic transformation you don't have to grow up in a black-and-white room. Ordinary people can have epistemic transformations with ordinary life experiences, and so may confront this under ordinary circumstances. A real-world epistemic transformation involving a relatively minor epistemic change might involve the experience of tasting a new kind of food. Think of a baby who tastes chocolate ice cream for the first time. Babies, with their relatively limited set of previous experiences, could have these sorts of epistemic transformations all the time—such transformations may be even be part of a successful developmental learning strategy (in a suitably safe environment).

The subjective value of an experience is assessed by knowing what it's like to have that experience. Once you've had an experience of the right sort, you have the knowledge you need to be able to make inferences about what similar future experiences will be like, and thus you have the knowledge you need to assign future subjective values of that type. What matters for this kind of inference is that you've had the right sort of experience in the past, because if you've had the right sort of experience, you can know quite a bit about the subjective value of future experiences of that type. This matters, because in many decisions, we are trying to assess what our future experiences could be like so that we can compare their subjective values.

Subjective values play an important role when we are making decisions if, when we evaluate our alternatives, we choose between them

[18] A priori physicalists think that, if we had complete physical information, we'd know what it was like to see red even without color experience. I'm not convinced. I think you *must* have the experience. But what I'm saying here does not depend on denying the a priori physicalist's claim: as I've made clear, I'm worried about what ordinary Mary can know, not about what Jackson's scientist Mary can know.

based on the expected subjective value of an act, determined in turn by the weighted subjective values of the experiential outcomes of our possible actions. When ordinary Mary has to choose whether to stay in her black-and-white room or to leave and experience color for the first time, she will want to know what her subjective value of seeing color will be. Unfortunately for her, because the experience will be epistemically transformative, she cannot know what it will be like for her to see color, and thus she cannot assign a subjective value to this future experience.

Ordinary circumstances can place us in a similar predicament. Consider one's first experience of tasting a durian fruit. The durian is known to have a foul smell but a delicious flavor. I've never tasted a durian, and because I've never tasted one or anything like one, I can't know what it is like to taste one—that is, I can't know what a durian tastes like. This isn't to say that I can't understand evocative statements about what it would be like to taste one—I can—but to truly grasp the subjective value of this experience, I have to have the experience itself. And thus, I can't assign a subjective value to the experience of tasting durian.

Until I taste the fruit of a durian, there's something I can't know— and that something is what it's like to taste a durian. When I taste it for the first time, by becoming acquainted with this taste, I'll undergo an epistemically transformative experience, and gain new knowledge, the knowledge of what it's like to taste a durian. The knowledge comes from the fact that, when I taste the durian, the intrinsic nature of having this type of taste experience is revealed to me, allowing me to grasp a new subjective value.[19]

Having new taste experiences is rather mundane in the grander scheme of things, even in (my rather less grand) purely personal scheme of things. For while I might find the experience of eating a durian intense, perhaps like some, finding it disgusting, or, like others, finding it ambrosial, the experience will not fundamentally change my self-defining preferences or my subjective point of view. If I'm to taste a durian in the next moment, I don't know what it will be like for me to taste it, but I still

---

[19] And, some might say, to grasp a new phenomenal fact.

know what it will be like to be *me* when I do taste it. New tastes can be wonderful, but they aren't the sorts of things that fundamentally change what you care about or what kind of person you take yourself to be.

The sorts of experiences that *can* change who you are, in the sense of radically changing your point of view (rather than only slightly modifying your preferences), are experiences that are *personally transformative*. Such experiences may include experiencing a horrific physical attack, gaining a new sensory ability, having a traumatic accident, undergoing major surgery, winning an Olympic gold medal, participating in a revolution, having a religious conversion, having a child, experiencing the death of a parent, making a major scientific discovery, or experiencing the death of a child. The experience can be life-changing in that it changes what it is like for you to be you. That is, it can change your point of view, and by extension, your personal preferences, and perhaps even change the kind of person that you are or at least take yourself to be. If an experience changes you enough to substantially change your point of view, thus substantially revising your core preferences or revising how you experience being yourself, it is a personally transformative experience.[20]

The inaccessibility of radically new experiences brings out the personal dimension of the fact I mentioned above, that what you can know at one time can be inaccessible to you at another time. Some personal

[20] After developing my account of personally transformative experience, I came across a lovely paper by Edna Ullmann-Margalit (2006), "Big decisions: opting, converting, drifting." She also points out that big decisions often involve substantial changes in one's subjective preferences, so that the person who makes the decision does not have the same preferences as the person who lives with the decision. She argues that to make the choice rational, we'd have to find a decision theoretic model that could represent our second-order preferences concerning our future selves: "The question I am raising is whether it is possible to assess the rationality of [t]his choice, given that this choice straddles two discontinuous personalities with two different rationality bases" (p. 13). Elster (1979) and Parfit (1984) describe similar cases. For personally transformative decisions involving forecastable preferences, I agree that we'd need this sort of model. But as I discuss later in this chapter, the real problem is much worse than this, because in cases that are both personally transformative and epistemically transformative, we can't know which future personal preferences we'd end up with, so we lack the knowledge we need to determine the right higher-order model.

transformations might be extensive, but also predictable, perhaps because you've undergone a similar transformation in the past. But if a personally transformative experience is a radically new experience for you, it means that important features of your future self, the self that results from the personal transformation, are epistemically inaccessible to your current, inexperienced self.[21] A radically new experience can fundamentally change your own point of view so much and so deeply that, before you've had that experience, you can't know what it is going to be like to be you after the experience. It changes your subjective value for what it is like to be you, and changes your core preferences about what matters.

This means that experiences, as I shall discuss them, have two ways of being transformative. They can be epistemically transformative, giving you new information in virtue of your experience. And they can be personally transformative, changing how you experience being who you are. Some experiences may be epistemically transformative while not being personally transformative, like tasting a durian for the first time. Some experiences may be personally transformative without being epistemically transformative.

The sort of case that is especially interesting, and the sort of case that is the focus of this book, involves an experience that is both epistemically *and* personally transformative. When I use the phrase "transformative experience" without qualification I will mean to pick out these sorts of experiences, the sorts of experiences that are both epistemically and personally transformative.

Having a transformative experience teaches you something new, something that you could not have known before having the experience, while also changing you as a person. Such experiences are very important from a personal perspective, for transformative experiences can play a significant role in your life, involving options that, speaking metaphorically, function as crossroads in your path towards self-realization.

---

[21] The epistemic inaccessibility of what it is like to lose a child, or to lose a spouse, or a parent, may be part of what underlies the resentment of the bereaved to comments (from those who have not experienced such a loss) along the lines of "I understand what you are going through."

The path you choose determines where you take your life, what you will become, and thus, by extension, your subjective future. Your own choices involving transformative experiences, that is, your *transformative choices*, allow you to causally form what it will be like to be you in your future. In this sense, you *own* your future, because it is *you* who made the choice to bring this future—your very own future self—into being.

Transformative experiences are also philosophically important. For, as I shall argue, they constitute a class of experiences that raise a special problem for decision-making, at least, for decision-making made from the subjective perspective of the individual.

The sort of decision I will be considering in the rest of this book is just this sort of decision, the sort of personal decision that you need to make at various points in your life, a decision about whether to undergo an experience that will change your life in a significant new way. Such a decision is ordinarily conducted from your subjective point of view, and involves the need for you to reflectively deliberate about how the result of your decision will determine your future experience. This doesn't mean that you must be some sort of egoist, caring only about yourself. It just means that the decision is the kind of personal decision that has no obvious or appealing way of approaching it if you don't take into account your personal preferences and point of view, for it essentially involves your subjective values and your subjective future.

It's also the sort of decision, I will argue, that in some sense *should* be made from your personal point of view. That is, in your deliberations, you should include considerations about what the lived experience involved in the choice would be like for you, because there is no better way to take your personal perspective and preferences into account, including your personal preferences about your future lived experience and about anything and anyone external to you.

As I will develop in detail below, the problem is that when you face a transformative choice, that is, a choice of whether to undergo an epistemically and personally transformative experience, you cannot rationally make this choice based on what you think the transformative experience will be like. That is, you cannot rationally choose to have the experience, nor can you rationally choose to avoid it, to the extent that your choice is based on your assessments of what the experience would be like and what this would imply about the subjective value of your future lived experience.

Of course, when we make our choices, we should always make them in concert with our best moral, legal, and empirical standards. But in the circumstances I am considering in this book, there is no obvious answer about what to decide, there is more than one acceptable way for people to act, and different people react to the experience in different ways. Moreover, there isn't some external reason that trumps or dominates your choice, making subjective deliberation irrelevant or unnecessary. Public policymakers or authoritarian rulers have not issued a decree on what your decision should be, and there are no moral or religious rules that determine just which act you should choose. Nor does the available scientific data determine how you should decide. As a result, the decision centrally involves your preferences concerning your future lived experience and the lived experiences of others close to you, or at least, such preferences cannot be eliminated from your deliberations without doing violence to the natural and ordinary way you want to make the choice.

Sometimes you need to subjectively deliberate because the decision is so small-scale and personal that it isn't the sort of thing that is legislated by public policy or rulers, or it isn't measurable at the scientific scale. And even with a big decision, sometimes the relevant legislation just doesn't exist, or there are cultural norms against legislating it, or the scientific data is inconclusive. And importantly for what follows, often, you want to subjectively deliberate about the choice simply because it's important to you to think about it and be the one to decide, since you care very much about how the outcome of this decision is going to affect your future and the futures of those you love.

## The Normative Standard

Ordinary decision-making at the personal level, to be rational, must follow the rules of a realistic normative decision theory. Normative decision theories present the most apt models for how people ought to make rational decisions, and realistic versions of these models provide guidelines that are applicable to real world cases.[22]

It is important to contrast normative decision theory with descriptive decision theory: descriptive decision theory is about the real world too, but it doesn't prescribe how agents in the real world *ought* to make decisions, if they are to be made rationally. Rather, descriptive decision theory describes how real people *actually* make their decisions, cataloguing their foibles and inclinations and mistakes, in order to understand the imperfect way actual people reason, and perhaps to develop corrective practices.[23]

My concern here is not descriptive. I'm not focusing on cases where, once ordinary people decide on what choice is the rational one, we must assess how good they are at actually following through with making this choice or how accurate they are in their thinking about the choice once they've made it.[24] I am looking at decision-making even before we get to that point. My concern is with cases where, *in principle*, we may not be able to make rational choices if we retain our ordinary perspective on subjective decision-making.

So the question I want to raise here is primarily normative: that is, I want to discuss whether it is even *possible* for real world agents to meet an acceptable rational, normative standard when making certain epistemically and personally transformative decisions from the subjective point of view.

An issue that will come up here and in later chapters involves our ability, as decision-makers, to get the information we need to make our decision. There are all kinds of ways in which our ability to get the

---

[22] Paul Weirich (2004) gives an excellent treatment in his *Realistic Decision Theory: Rules for Nonideal Agents in Nonideal Circumstances*.

[23] See, for example, Gilbert (2007), Wilson (2011), Kahneman (2013).

[24] It is well known that we are, at least with respect to certain kinds of personal decisions, not especially good at making these decisions the way we should make them if we were acting as rationally as we could, nor at assessing the values of the outcomes we previously decided to bring about, nor even at recalling the details

needed information can be compromised: humans might not have the mental capacities needed to do the mathematical calculation, the science involved might not be advanced enough, it might be too expensive to get the information we need, or it might be so complicated or physically difficult to get the information that, for all intents and purposes, we can't get it.

What we want to know, given the sorts of limitations we face, is how we should reason. In particular, the question we will consider is, how should we, as individuals who are intelligent and capable reasoners in ordinary circumstances, finding ourselves in a situation where we have only limited access to certain kinds of facts, proceed rationally when making decisions about our subjective futures? In other words, what are the normative constraints on our reasoning, if we are to deliberate and choose to act rationally, when we are in this sort of situation?

Normative decision theory, in this context, is important because when we make decisions, we want to make them rationally, at least as rationally as we can, and normative decision theory gives us the models and the principles for the procedures we should follow—as some describe it, it is "action-guiding."

The normative standard for rational decision-making is that the agent or decision-maker should choose the act that has the highest expected value. The idea is that, when you are to decide what you want to do in a normatively rational way, you should proceed by determining the probabilities of the relevant states of the world, that, combined with your possible act, will bring about the relevant outcomes. You also determine the values of the possible outcomes of your possible acts, and, after weighting these values, determine which act you should perform in order to maximize your expected value.[25]

of our past experiences, or remembering why we chose the act we did. Gilbert (2007), Wilson (2011), and Kahneman (2013) discuss these issues very nicely.

[25] For simplicity, in this context, I will take agents to have preferences that reflect their value functions, and will assume that the values or utilities assigned to outcomes are psychologically real for the agent (even if, for example, utilities

When you want to make a rational choice between relevant alternatives, then, you must grasp, at least approximately and implicitly, the facts about the way to act that best fits your preferences.[26]

What counts as valuable for you when making a particular choice will depend on your dispositions, beliefs, and desires. In the standard case, the best choice for the normatively rational decision-maker is to choose to perform the act with the highest expected value, given her assignments of values to outcomes and probabilities to states, where the expected value of the act is determined by multiplying the values of the outcomes by the probabilities of the states and then adding these values together. A standard way to describe these outcomes is in terms of one's *rational expectations*, but I will find it more appropriate in what follows to describe outcomes in terms of "what it is like," such as *knowing what it is like to be a vampire* or in terms of what it's like to have certain experiences.

Your degrees of belief about the probabilities of various states are measures of the degrees to which you expect the world to be a certain way, and are called your *credences*.[27] We can speak loosely of assigning credences or probabilities to outcomes, where that is understood more precisely as a function of the credences or probabilities assigned to the states of the world that, together with acts, generate the outcomes.

An issue here involves the evidence we, as the decision-makers, have when we are assigning values to outcomes and credences to states of the world in order to calculate the expected values of our actions. If we are to meet the normative standard when we make our choices, we

turn out to be partially constituted by their role in preferences). See the discussion of psychological realism in Buchak (2016).

[26] As Paul Weirich noted to me, there can be differences between the method an agent uses for making a choice and the method she uses for evaluating a choice. I am eliding these differences for simplicity.

[27] In what follows, I will often speak of credences, that is, subjective degrees of belief, instead of speaking about probabilities, and for the purposes of this discussion, I will assume probabilism, which says that our credences at a given time ought to satisfy the axioms of the probability calculus. But my conclusions hold even if probabilism and talk of credences is eschewed.

must be rationally justified in our assignments of values and credences to the outcomes and states of our decision problem. That is, we must assign our values and credences based on sufficient evidence. If we assign values and credences based on insufficient evidence, and calculate the expected value of our acts using such assignments, our decision does not meet the normative standard for rationality. The lunatic in the asylum who sees ghosts in every corner and assigns values and credences on that basis does not meet the normative standard, even if he acts in a way that, by his lights, would maximize his expected value.

The reason why the normative standard is important to us, even practically, is because we want to know how reliably we, as decision-makers, can hope to meet this standard in our decision-making. I am especially interested in exploring the way we should regard and navigate deeply personal, centrally important, life-changing decisions, given the desirability of meeting the normative standard in such cases. Major life decisions determine our personal futures, and centrally concern what it will be like for us to experience the futures we make for ourselves and those we care about. They are some of our most important decisions, and as such, whether we can even come close to reliably meeting the normative standard is hugely important.[28]

Examining the ways that experience relates to decision-making raises a related question: what do we have to know in order to guide rational action? Since we are interested in understanding, how, in principle, our decision-making should be action-guiding, that is, we want to know how, in principle, we should be making decisions about

---

[28] Compare discussions of norms in moral philosophy: for example, Kwame Anthony Appiah (2008, pp. 22–3) argues that "moral philosophy…must attend, in articulating and defending norms, to how they can come to bear in actual lives." And Owen Flanagan (1991), in *Varieties of Moral Personality*, defends the Principle of Minimal Psychological Realism: make sure when constructing a moral theory or projecting a moral ideal that the character, decision processing, and behavior prescribed are possible, or [factively] perceived to be possible, for creatures like us.

how to act, we are interested in the connections between knowledge, belief, reasons, and action.

Some philosophers have argued that knowledge is necessary to have a reason for action, and so if you do not know a certain proposition, then you should not use this proposition as a reason for rational action.[29] Others have argued that if you lack the relevant knowledge, you lack the abilities you need to guide rational action.[30]

We can see the focus on experience and decision-making as raising a different, but related problem. If you think you cannot know what it is like to have a certain experience because you cannot grasp this information in the relevant way, you might think you cannot entertain facts or propositions with *what it's like to see red* as a constituent because you cannot grasp these facts or propositions in the relevant way.[31] And if you cannot even entertain a certain fact or proposition, much less know it, then you cannot use it as an evidence-based reason or guide for rational action. Framed in this way, we can see how the sort of epistemic impoverishment resulting from limited experience could put even more severe constraints on one's ability to act rationally than cases where one doesn't know where the restaurant is, or whether the barn across the field is real.

## Subjective Deliberation

As I've been emphasizing, the focus here is on subjective decision-making. This is the kind of decision-making that is made from one's first personal point of view. It involves the sorts of decisions we make all the time for ourselves. It is not merely subjective in the sense of being a decision made by an individual about her own

---

[29] Hawthorne and Stanley (2008). Related discussion comes up in Fantl and McGrath (2002).

[30] See, for example, Unger (1975); Hyman (1999); and Littlejohn (2012).

[31] Here, for simplicity, I am simply assuming that "what it's like" clauses denote facts or propositions.

future, it is subjective in the sense of being phenomenological, that is, it is subjective in the sense of being a deliberation about how to act that is conducted from one's first personal, phenomenally conscious perspective. This means that, as I consider life's big decisions from a normative decision-theoretic perspective, I am especially interested in cases where we want to make a rational choice between relevant alternatives by determining how to act in a way that will have the highest expected subjective value.

What I am committed to is the importance of exploring this sort of deliberation from the subjective perspective, that is, from the first personal, psychological point of view, where we assess different subjective values of outcomes that might arise from various acts we could perform. It is worth noting that this approach dovetails with a predominant cultural paradigm of how to approach decisions about our own lives. According to that paradigm, we approach many major life decisions as personal matters where a central feature of what is at stake is what it will be like for us to experience the outcomes of our acts, and where the subjective value we assign to an outcome depends upon what we care about, whatever that might be.

The subjective value of outcomes matters to us even if, for example, we care most about the outcome's moral status, for the subjective value we assign to that outcome will be reflected in what it is like for us to experience that outcome as morally important.[32] Of course, an outcome will also have nonsubjective value, for example, it may have objective moral value, and this could affect the expected value of the act that could bring it about. But I am setting these other sorts of values aside for now, in order to focus on the subjective values of outcomes, and thus to focus on our assessment of the expected subjective value of our acts. (When I use the term "value" in the chapters that follow, I mean "subjective value" unless I explicitly or contextually specify otherwise.)

---

[32] Recall that subjective value attaches to lived experience, and that I am assuming that we are not hallucinating, or in an experience-generating machine, or otherwise seriously deceived.

While subjective values are not the only values of these outcomes, they are some of the most central and important ones, and an emphasis on them fits the dominant cultural paradigm. Rather amazingly, they have been neglected by contemporary "analytic" philosophy.

Subjective decision-making is especially important when we find ourselves at certain critical junctions in our lives, times when we need to make a major decision about who we want to become and how we want to get there. At such a junction, we mentally stop and evaluate the different choices we can make—that is, we project forward and evaluate different possible acts and their outcomes—judging each act and contrasting it to the others, ideally selecting the act that that maximizes our expected subjective value.

The outcomes we are considering here are experiential, in that they are described by "what it's like" locutions—they are outcomes such as what it is like to taste a durian or what it is like to be a vampire.[33] A way to think about how we assess the subjective values of possible experiences is to represent ourselves as engaging in a kind of cognitive modeling. When you are considering your options, you evaluate each possible act and its experiential outcomes by imagining or running a mental simulation of what it would be like, should you act, for each relevant possible outcome of each relevant act. You simulate the relevant possible outcomes for yourself, that is, you simulate what it would be like for you to have each of these experiences and what your life would be like after these experiences.[34]

---

[33] Again, the outcomes are not *merely* phenomenological. For example, I am assuming that we are considering cases where, if the outcome is realized, the phenomenology would be grounded by the relevant state: you really are tasting a durian, or you really are a vampire. Phenomenology isn't the only thing that matters—but it does matter!

[34] As I noted above, a more traditional way of describing these outcomes might be in terms of our *expectations*, for example, in terms of our rational expectations about the experience of being a vampire. My arguments will go through if formulated in terms of rational expectations, but I find other locutions more natural in this discussion.

After you run each cognitive simulation, you assign each outcome a subjective value. This value may be based partly on what you judge the qualitative phenomenal value of the outcome to be, that is, on the value of what it would be like for you, purely in terms of qualitative phenomenological character, if that outcome were to occur. But, as I made clear above, you are also taking nonqualitative content to be part of your cognitive phenomenology and thus to be represented by what it is like for you. In particular, your moral and religious beliefs, your belief that your perceptions are veridical, your beliefs and attitudes in response to social practices and norms, and any other relevant cognitive features will also be represented by your cognitive phenomenology, and thus will be part of what you use to determine the subjective value for each of your experiential outcomes. Once you've determined the overall subjective value of each outcome, you can compare the expected values of different possible acts to determine which one you should perform.

This raises a question: do subjective values involve practical reasons? Yes, if we think these reasons are represented in one's conscious experience. As such, they can feed into the subjective values we assign.[35]

One of the main reasons why, when we face decisions, we run cognitive simulations, is to discover how we want to value possible outcomes. Sometimes we can know how to act without running the simulations. For example, you can know that being eaten by a shark will be horrible, even without running cognitive simulations

---

[35] Although I'm not committed to any particular view of practical reason, Gibbons (2010) argues convincingly that we should take practical reasons to be psychological in this way. In this discussion, however, I am not taking a position on this view, nor on whether moral deliberation is a form of rational deliberation, or whether its aim is to maximize value, and I'm not too concerned about what counts as a "practical reason." If you reject the psychological approach towards practical reasons, then take my discussion to be merely about our predominant cultural paradigm of how to approach certain very important decisions about our own lives.

to determine what it would be like. You can know that getting your legs amputated without anesthesia would be painful, even without exploring the contours of that particular cognitive model. But if you are not sure how you'd respond to an experience, perhaps because there is wide variation in the way that different people respond to it, or because you have reason to suppose that you will respond differently from most, or perhaps because the situation is unique enough that general principles or known facts do not entail what you should think about the results, you'll want to run simulations to determine subjective values for yourself, that is, to determine what you think different possible outcomes would be like, in order to determine how to act. (For the rest of this book, unless I note otherwise, I will be setting aside decisions like the decision to avoid swimming with sharks, that is, I'm setting aside decision contexts like these where there is no need to deliberate by cognitively modeling in order to assess the subjective value of the relevant outcomes.)

Built into the way you assess expected values is another factor: your assessment of the probability of the state of the world needed for an outcome to occur, should you perform the relevant act. You attach a probability to the world being in the relevant possible state, so that you can calculate the act's expected value, which is a function of the values of its possible outcomes and the probabilities that the world is a certain way.

This brings out another complication that ordinary decision-makers face. Often, the world only gives you incomplete or partial information about the probabilities associated with the relevant states of the world. In particular, you might not know how likely a particular state is.

If you can't know the probability you should attach to a relevant state, but you have to choose anyway, then you will need to make a decision even though you suffer from a certain kind of *ignorance*—ignorance of the relevant probabilities. Despite this, in many cases, you can choose rationally if you can follow a standard normative model for decision-making under ignorance when you make your choice. Standard models for these situations are models designed for situations when we don't know some or all of the probabilities of the relevant states that, given the right act, would lead to the outcomes of interest, yet we still want to choose rationally, given the information that we do have.[36]

To see how standard models handle such situations, it is important to distinguish carefully between the two major parts of the structure represented by a decision-theoretic model: the values of the outcomes, and the probability that the state needed for each outcome will occur, given that the act needed to bring it about occurs. A decision involving ignorance of the sort we are considering is a situation where the values of the relevant outcomes are known, but the agent doesn't know all the probabilities of the states. The agent's ignorance is reflected by the fact that certain probability assignments are missing in the model.

What standard models for decision under ignorance give us is a way to manage a situation when we know what the relevant act, outcome, and value structure of the problem is, that is, when we know what acts we are considering, what the relevant possible outcomes and their values are, and how these values compare, but we don't know the probabilities attaching to the states of the world needed for these outcomes to occur. If we don't know the probabilities, we can't calculate the expected value of an act, so we need to find another way to decide how to act. A model for decision under ignorance can represent the structure of the tradeoffs we should be willing to make, given our dispositions and what we know about the respective values of the relevant possible outcomes of our choices. For example, if we are risk-seeking (or perhaps just not risk-averse), we might be willing to act in a way that makes it possible for the highest-value outcome to occur, even if we don't know how likely it is that the state needed for that outcome will obtain. If we

---

[36] For simplicity, and because, in this context, we are considering ordinary individuals (like ordinary Mary from above), throughout the text I will elide irrelevant differences between knowing, being rationally justified in assigning, assessing, grasping, and determining. In particular, when we consider ignorance of utilities below, the point is that, without the relevant experience, an ordinary person cannot know, cannot rationally assign, cannot grasp, cannot assess and cannot determine the subjective value in the relevant, first-personal, imaginative sense.

are risk-averse, we might be willing to act in a way that makes it impossible for the lowest-value outcome to occur, even if we don't know how likely it is that the state needed for that outcome will obtain.

Models for decision-making under ignorance represent a structure that can be used to guide rational action, and their appeal can be indexed to the personality type of the person who is making the choice. The models can be used to represent different attitudes towards risk in an agent so that the agent who follows these models can choose how to act, all things considered, consistent with her level of risk aversion towards ways the world might turn out.[37] An acceptable normative model can represent this structure and provide a decision-theoretic guide to many sorts of complex subjective decisions.[38]

## Transformative Decisions

The key to understanding the problem that transformative experience raises is to recognize that the standard models for ignorance can only function if they can represent the structure of the value space of the outcomes for a decision problem. This is because they function by modeling the relationships between the values of the outcomes of different choices, helping us to see how to choose in a way that respects the tradeoffs we should make when we don't know enough about the actual world to factor in probabilities.

As a result, in order to use these models for a decision made under conditions of ignorance, *you must be able to know the values of the relevant outcomes*. You do not need to know the probabilities that the outcomes, given the acts, will occur, but you do need to know how to value the relevant outcomes. A way to put this is that you must be able to describe the state space of your outcomes, and you must have a suitably defined value function for these outcomes. If you cannot

---

[37] See Buchak (2014) for an excellent discussion of agents' attitudes towards risk.

[38] Weirich, *Realistic Decision Theory*.

know the values of the relevant outcomes or if the values are not yet determined, so that you cannot describe the state space or assign values that will remain constant to outcomes, you do not have the information you need to use these types of models to represent your decision. For without an adequate description of the space and without a suitably defined value function for the outcomes, you cannot know if the structure of any particular model adequately represents the structure of the actual situation.

For example, if you are risk-averse and want to act in a way that precludes the possibility of the worst outcome occurring, you need to know what the values of the outcomes are, that is, just *how* good or bad each of the outcomes is, relative to the others, in order to know which one is the worst, or lowest-value, one. Similarly, if you are risk-seeking, you need to know how good or bad the values of the outcomes are, in order to compare the relative values of the relevant outcomes to know which is the best, or highest-value, one.

And if you cannot determine what the values of the outcomes are—no matter whether you cannot know for principled epistemic reasons or for practical reasons contingent on the limited facts available to you in that situation—on the standard normative model, you are not rationally justified in assigning values to the outcomes. You lack the evidence you need to be rationally justified in making such assignments.

And even if you can know something about the outcomes, such as the range of the values for the outcomes, if you cannot grasp the different values in the relevant way you need to in order to compare them, you cannot determine the relevant structure of the relationships between the values. Without this information about what the values are and how they compare to each other, standard models for decision under ignorance are of no help to the decision-maker.

This is precisely the problem for normative decision-making involving transformative experiences. As I described above, when you face a transformative choice, that is, a choice of whether to undergo an epistemically and personally transformative experience, you face a certain kind of ignorance: ignorance about what it will be like to undergo the experience and ignorance about how the experience will change you. Thus, you face a certain kind of ignorance about what your future will be like.

To apply a normative decision-theoretic model for ignorance to a decision about whether to perform an act, you need to know the values of the relevant outcomes, including their relative strengths, and you must be able to compare the values of the outcomes in order to determine the overall structure of the value space.

But in the case of a decision involving a transformative experience, you cannot know what it is like to have that kind of experience until you've had it.[39] In this situation, you cannot determine the subjective value of any outcome that involves what it is like for you to have or have had that experience. And if you cannot determine the subjective values of the relevant outcomes, you cannot compare the values. In this situation, you are like the agent who cannot rationally determine the value of winning the lottery because he cannot determine the value of the prize, so he cannot decide whether he should pay to play.[40]

And the problem is doubly serious, for not only do you not know the values before you've had the relevant experience, but having the experience can change your preferences, and so the values you would (per impossibile) assign these outcomes before having the transformative experience could be radically different from the values you'd assign to the relevant outcomes after having had the experience. So because you don't know what the experience is like, you don't know how your preferences will change as the result of having the transformative experience.

In such a situation, you cannot apply standard decision-theoretic models for ignorance. The models don't apply because your ignorance, at least in the first instance, is not just about the probabilities—it's about the values. And the problem isn't one of uncertainty

[39] I am assuming, here and throughout, that cases like the shark-eating case are outside of the scope of this discussion.

[40] Weirich (2004, p. 65).

about the values, it's that, when we are supposed to choose, we *cannot know* the relevant values, either because our pre-choice self cannot assign them or because they will change in unknown ways.[41] (In the Afterword, using the example of choosing to have a child, I show how models for agents with imprecise credences can't be used to circumvent this problem, and I discuss work by Alan Hájek and Harris Nover on the decision-theoretic problems raised by games with indeterminate values.) It would seem that decisions involving transformative experiences that are made based on one's subjective values are simply outside the scope of decision theory. That is, it would seem that decision theory simply doesn't apply, so *it doesn't make sense to ask how agents should rationally make transformative decisions.*

Now, in fact, I think it does make sense to ask how rational agents should make transformative decisions, because I think agents *can* meet the relevant normative standard. So, in the end, I will argue that normative decision theory does apply. But there is a catch: in order for standard decision theory to apply, we will have to reject or significantly modify a deeply ingrained, very natural approach to making such decisions, the approach that takes subjective values of one's future lived experience into account. Recognizing that these decisions need to be reformulated, and understanding the consequences of this for the way we should regard our plans and decisions about our subjective futures, is the central focus of this book.

The problem to address in cases of transformative choice is that, given the way the decision is naturally framed, you lack the ability to rationally determine the subjective values of the relevant outcomes, both because you cannot assign them at the outset and because the experience will change you in ways unknown.

And so, in general, with transformative choices, you cannot get to the point you'd need to be at in order to make a (potentially) rational choice, because you cannot determine the relevant values. For

---

[41] So the problem isn't that, for example, we know the values but aren't certain about how to order them, sort them, or compare them.

example, in a case where you must choose between becoming a vampire or remaining human, the problem is not that you know that the values of the outcomes of these acts are incomparable, or are equal but different in some way. Nor is the situation one where, once you've determined the values of the outcomes, you simply choose between acts with expected values that are equally good (or equally bad), or you pick between acts with the same expected value based on other considerations.[42] Rather, before becoming a vampire, you cannot determine the subjective value of becoming a vampire at all, and thus you cannot, even in principle, make the right sorts of value-based comparisons. In such a case, you are being asked to consider the possibility of an outcome where you, as the human making the decision, cannot even construct a rationally defensible evaluation of what it would be like to live your life in this way. [43]

---

[42] If you cannot determine the expected value of an act, you cannot have value-based reasons for choosing that act, and so you cannot use these reasons to guide your reasoning about that act in a way that falls within the scope of normatively rational decision-making.

[43] Joseph Raz argues that in a case where we know enough about the values we assign to outcomes to know that they are not comparable or incommensurable, we can still have sufficient reason to prefer one outcome over the other. In such a case, say, a choice between a career as a lawyer or a career as a clarinetist, choosing either is rationally permissible. Ruth Chang (2012), in "Are hard choices cases of incomparability?", criticizes his approach, arguing that values must be comparable in order for reason to guide action and choice. In my cases, however, the problem comes from the fact that we cannot even determine or assign the values (and so we cannot even know whether or how the values are comparable). Raz's (1988, p. 329) view is designed to apply to cases where we can assign values to outcomes, but we know these values are incomparable or incommensurable. "Statements of incommensurability, i.e., statements that of two options neither is better nor are they of equal value, do not compare the value of options. They are denials that their values are comparable. Incommensurability is not yet another valuation of the relative merits of two options alongside such valuations as having greater value or having equal value. It is a rejection of the applicability of such judgments to the options in question." Related issues come up concerning picking between acts with equivalent expected values in Ullmann-Margalit and Morgenbesser (1977).

We can see the way decision-theoretic models will fail in contexts where we cannot know the relevant values by mapping out some examples in more detail. Start with our durian example. Imagine that you are in Thailand for the first time, considering whether to have pineapple or durian for breakfast. We can assume that you enjoy pineapple, but it isn't your favorite fruit. If the pineapple is ripe, you know it will probably resemble previous experiences you've had eating pineapple, and that you'll enjoy having it about as much as you have in the past. So, because you know what it is like to eat pineapple, you can rationally assign a moderately high positive subjective value to the experience of eating it.

But if you've never had a durian, you don't know what it will be like for you to taste one, and you cannot know what it is like until you try it. Moreover, people seem to have very different reactions to the durian fruit—enjoying a durian isn't just a matter of having sophisticated tastes, or simply liking exotic fruit. While many famous chefs absolutely love it, some find it repulsive. Anthony Bourdain describes it thus: "Its taste can only be described as…indescribable, something you either love or despise. And then afterwards your breath will smell as if you'd been French-kissing your dead grandmother." Tim Anderson, another chef, notes that "Some people say it smells like dead rats."[44] So even if you love to try new foods, there is a range of possible subjective values, from positive to negative, that you could assign to the outcome of what it is like to eat a durian. Finally, the value of the outcome is partially determined by the phenomenal intensity of what it is like for you to taste a durian, and so the magnitude of the positive or negative subjective value is not just determined by the fact that the durian tastes good (or bad) to you, but by how intense your taste experience is.

Because the taste of the durian has not been revealed to you through your experience, you cannot assign a subjective value to the experiential

---

[44] *New York Daily News*, "World's stinkiest fruit is turned into wine," July 2013; and *The Guardian*, "Durian, the world's smelliest fruit, goes on sale in Britain," February 3, 2014.

outcome of what it is like to eat it.[45] So you can't evaluate the choice to have a durian in terms of a comparison between the taste of pineapple and the taste of durian. Since you don't know the possible values for tasting durian, you don't know enough about the structure of the values of the outcome space to use a standard model for decision-making under ignorance to make a choice organized around these outcomes.

The problem posed by epistemically transformative experiences for decision-making is not a problem that arises in virtue of the fact that *any* experience may—in some way—be qualitatively new or different from your past experiences. For example, you may have tasted ripe pineapple in the past, and so you know what the experience of tasting ripe pineapple is like, broadly speaking. But you may not know what it will be like to taste *this* piece of pineapple in front of you. Perhaps it will be ever so slightly acidic. Or perhaps it will be cloyingly sweet. Perhaps as a result it'll taste a tiny bit different from any other piece of ripe pineapple that you've had in the past. Does this fact create a problem for your breakfast decision?

No. Epistemically transformative experiences arise from having new *kinds* of experiences, not from new token experiences that are instances of the kinds of experiences you already know about. If you've had an experience of a particular kind already, you know enough about its dominant, that is, its kind-defining, properties to know what having an experience of that kind is like. This is because you already know what it's like to experience those kind-defining properties. (Of course, you could make a mistake: the piece of ripe pineapple or your experience of it might not have the kind-defining properties it is supposed to. Here we are assuming you have enough evidence to know which kind the experience will be.) Minor changes or variations in properties that are not the dominant, kind-defining properties of the experience are not relevant to knowing what that kind of experience is like.

---

[45] And remember, current science doesn't pronounce on how you'll respond, and experiences vary widely, so you can't rely on testimony. (And we are setting aside sci-fi cases where a perfect duplicate of you tries it and somehow tells you what subjective values to assign, etc.)

That it is *kinds* of experiences that matter here is reflected in the fineness of grain of the decision procedure: I just need to know what it's like to taste ripe pineapple in general, so that I can use what I know to assign a subjective value to the outcome involving a possible instance of that experience-kind.

Now, the objection can be refined, of course. It's true that you know what it's like to taste ripe pineapple. But if you've never had the experience of tasting ripe-pineapple-with-just-this-amount-of-cloying-sweetness-and-acidity, you are still having a new kind of experience when you taste the piece of pineapple in front of you. It's just an experience of a highly specific new kind: the new kind described by "ripe-pineapple-with-just-this-amount-of-cloying-sweetness-and-acidity." This specific kind is not a natural or ordinary kind. But more importantly, the experiential properties that define it as a kind, highly specific properties such as just *this* amount of cloying sweetness and just *that* much acidity are not of much interest in most decision-making situations, and the way we formulate and evaluate outcomes reflects this.[46] So while it is true that I might have to actually taste this very piece of pineapple before I can know precisely what it tastes like, my lack of interest in instances of this highly refined kind, and correspondingly, the lowness of the stakes involved, make the new information discovered with this epistemically transformative experience irrelevant. Lacking this sort of information is not what is stopping you from rationally deciding what to have for breakfast in our Thailand example.

One thing you might do to make the choice between pineapple and durian rational is reconfigure the decision. We can know that certain types of new experiences won't affect us that much, and so, for that sort of new experience, we can know the approximate range of possible subjective values. The way we grasp the range of the values isn't by knowing what it would be like to have the experience, but by

---

[46] Obviously, this does not impugn the fact that in some decision-making contexts we could in fact care about highly refined kinds like this.

knowing enough about a higher-order fact about that type of experience to know that there is a low limit on how positive a value for that experience could be (and a low limit on how negative the value could be). Trying durian seems to be like this—after all, it's just trying a new kind of fruit. You've had fruit before. How good (or bad) could the experience of tasting this new fruit be?

So you might revise your choice, changing the outcomes you base your decision to act upon, so that the relevant outcome of choosing durian is not the experience of what it's like to taste a durian, but the experience of tasting a new fruit, whatever it is like. You could forgo eating durian simply on the grounds that you don't want to risk having a bad fruit experience. Or, you might decide to try eating durian just for the sake of having had the experience of eating durian (so you can report back to your friends "I've tried it!"). The relevant subjective value, then, is the revelatory value of discovering the intrinsic nature of the experience of tasting durian.

One way to revise the decision, then, would be to base it on the outcomes of *knowing what it is like to taste durian* versus *not knowing what it is like to taste durian*, and attach values that reflect the value of having this new knowledge, whether the taste is good or bad. Another way to revise is to frame the decision in terms of the expected value of an act with an outcome such as *having the experience of tasting this new kind of fruit* versus the expected value of an act with the outcome of *avoiding the experience of tasting this new kind of fruit*. In either reformulation, you can then assign values that reflect the subjective value of having the revelation or avoiding the revelation.

Trying a durian, or forgoing a durian, simply on the basis of the expected subjective value of trying it (or forgoing it) is a way to reconfigure the decision to make it rational. Instead of constructing the decision in terms of what it's like to taste a durian, you can choose to try the durian based on whether you want to have a new fruit experience for its own sake, that is, solely for the expected value of discovering the intrinsic nature of this type of experience, good or bad. The tradeoff, then, is structured in terms of choices between acts with outcomes with known subjective values based on what it's like to taste pineapple and acts with outcomes with known subjective values based on the value of discovering a new kind of taste.

If you reconfigure the decision like this, your choice is framed as a choice of whether to have a new kind of experience solely for the sake of discovering the information carried by having that kind of experience. The value of making your decision this way is that it allows you to use normative decision-theoretic models to represent the structure of the decision-making process.

This works well for relatively safe environments where we know not much is at stake. (I am assuming you know not much is at stake in the durian case because you know a lot about fruit, given your previous experience, and you know a durian is a fruit.) In such cases, we can try new experiences for the sake of their newness, knowing that a bad experience would exact a relatively low cost. If transformative experiences merely involved minor life events like trying a new fruit, or other sorts of cases that didn't affect us much, we could simply note the need to formulate decisions in terms of revelation in cases involving epistemically transformative experiences and move on. But transformative experiences are not restricted to minor life events.

Return to the example where neuroscientists and engineers invent a microchip that gives humans an interesting new sensory ability. We can imagine that, instead of simply adding a new sensory ability to the abilities you already have, when the new chip is implanted, it permanently eliminates your sense of taste just as it adds the new sense ability. (The brain's neural networks just can't support both abilities at the same time.) We can also assume that, if you choose to do it, you will be the first person to get the chip implanted.

The sort of choice you are considering is a choice between discovering a new kind of sensory ability in place of the ability to taste, versus having the ability to taste instead of discovering a new kind of sensory ability. The revelation involved is the discovery of the intrinsic nature of a new type of sense experience, and the subjective value of making this discovery (whether it be it a good, bad, or indifferent experience), would be traded off against the subjective value of being able to taste.

In this case, how should you decide whether to get the chip? If you can't know what it is like to have the new sensory ability, you can't compare it to what it is like for you to have the ability to taste in order to decide which one you prefer. The problem, again, is that you cannot know what it is like to have the new sensory ability, and thus you cannot know its subjective value. If you can't know this value, you don't know enough about the tradeoff between the ability to taste and the new sensory ability to know whether it's a trade you'd want to make.

What if, like in the durian case, you know that the new sensory ability could only be so good or so bad, that is, what if you know the range for the subjective values of having the new sense? After all, you have other sensory capacities, so you know about sensory experiences in a general way. Could you then make sense of a rational choice in terms of a tradeoff between keeping your sense of taste versus the subjective value of having a new sensory ability, whatever it's like?

Unfortunately, the parallel with the durian case fails. Until you know what it's like to have the new sensory experiences, you can't even know how to compare the subjective values associated with the ability to taste and the new sensory ability. And without this information, you can't know what to think about a tradeoff between taste experiences and the new sensory experiences. And sensory modalities can be linked, which means that the types of changes you might experience could extend past your limited general knowledge about sensory capacities, such that what it's like to experience the new combination of your previous and new sense modalities might significantly change how you'd value the outcomes, even apart from the way discovering the intrinsic natures of the new sense experiences could change your preferences. This case can't be solved the way the durian case can.

What the worry about comparability and changes in preferences really brings out is that, without actually knowing what it is like to have the new sensory ability, there isn't any useful sense in which you can determine the range of the values of having it. Knowing what it is like to have the new sense is precisely what determines your judgment of how bad or how good it would be, from your point of view, to have it replace your sense of taste. You need to know what it is like to have this sensory ability in order to be able to determine the range of the relevant subjective values, you need to know what it is like in order to know how to compare it to the subjective value of your ability to taste, and you need to know what *you'll* be like after the experience to know how you'll value the experiential outcomes at that time. The experience of having a new sense is simply too radically different from your previous experiences, and too life-changing, for you to be able to assess the nature, range and tradeoffs of the subjective values involved before you know what it is like.

And note that the disanalogy isn't just with range and comparability. For as I've been emphasizing, in a transformative experience like the chip case, the revelation involved changes one's preferences. In other words, when making the choice about whether to have the microchip, even if I reformulate it like I did in the durian case, I face the problem that, simply in virtue of the transformative nature of having this new sense experience, *my core preferences will be revised.* Before having the chip, perhaps I assign a low value to revelation, since I love good food and fine wine. But if I were to get chipped, I'd assign revelation a high value, embracing the new, tasteless me. When assessing what to do, which preferences trump? Which ones am I supposed to use to make my decision?

The chip case shows how, in general, when deliberating about life-changing experiences, we can't simply fudge things the way we did in the durian case, where we were reformulating a decision that was ultimately of little consequence. With major life experiences, the range of subjective values can be very large indeed, and we cannot simply assume that the best and worst outcomes will not have significant overall effects on our subjective futures. And since these life-changing experiences are dramatically new, that is, since they are transformative, we cannot assume that what we don't know about the nature of the new experience won't matter. That is, the new experience can affect the way we represent the comparative structure of the value space in a significant, surprising way, for example, by replacing the preferences that our old, pre-experience self had with new preferences, or by revealing that the values of the revelatory outcomes swamp the values of other subjective values. Moreover, since we don't even know how the subjective values of the different major life experiences we are trading off are to be compared, we might even discover that there is no possibility of modeling the decision using a coherent value structure at all. So the fact that we cannot know the subjective values of transformative experiences until we actually have the experiences has considerable traction in a context of transformative choice.

We have seen that we can't straightforwardly apply standard decision-theoretic models for ignorance to epistemically transformative cases, and that even if we reformulate the decisions to accommodate the models in an epistemically transformative case, cases that are both epistemically and personally transformative are still problematic. This matters, for many different kinds of major life events can be transformative, and the more major the life event is the more likely it is to be both epistemically and personally transformative.

In chapter 1, I considered the choice of whether to become a vampire as an example of a life-changing decision about one's future. It's worth exploring this case in a bit more detail to see how the worries play out, now that we see the deep structure of the decision problem. Focus your attention on the relevant issues by considering a version of the vampire case where your choice is basically up to you, such that it centrally involves your personal perspective, and there are no dominant objective moral or other third personal considerations that determine the right choice. In other words, as with many big, personal decisions about how to map one's future, we are thinking of this case as a decision concerning a personal matter where a primary concern is your own expected future and the way you want to subjectively realize your life's goals.

There is a wide range of possible subjective values, from positive to negative, that you could assign to the outcome of becoming a vampire. The subjective value of what it will be like for you to become Undead is determined by how good or how bad your overall experience will be, and the range of possible values is enormous. This is true in part because the value of the outcome is partially determined by the phenomenal intensity of what it is like for you to become a vampire, and so a positive or negative subjective value is not just determined by the experience of being a vampire, but by how intense the experience is. There is the very real possibility that the phenomenal intensity of one of the outcomes, such as the phenomenal intensity of what it is like to be inhumanly powerful or the phenomenal intensity of craving blood, will swamp the rest of them. That is, the value of the phenomenally intense outcome could be so much higher or lower than the other outcomes that, for all intents and purposes, the other outcomes won't matter. Finally, given the transformative nature of becoming a vampire, many of your preferences, once you are a vampire, will be different from those you have as a human. So until you actually become a vampire, you cannot know if the values of any of the relevant outcomes will swamp the rest, or how to compare the subjective value of being a vampire to the subjective value of being human, or which preferences about the outcomes that you'd have as a vampire will be the same as the preferences you have as a human.

As the story went, all of your friends have become vampires, and all of them love it. Everyone who has done it tells you it is fantastic. Yet, even if, morally speaking, the animal blood you'd live on is no worse than eating a cheeseburger made from humanely farmed cows, and even if you'd cut a fabulous figure in black clothing, there is still something repulsive and frightening about becoming a member of the Undead. Moreover, it is an irreversible decision, so you can't just try it and go back to being human if you don't like it. Once you go immortal, you can never go back.

So, how should you think about the choice? You've never had a previous experience that actually resembled being a vampire, so you can't evaluate this outcome by reflecting on similar experiences. If

43

you've never been a vampire, you don't know what it will be like for you to be one, and you can't know unless you try it.

You might try to learn about what it is like to be a vampire by gracefully gliding around in a black cloak, staying up all night, sleeping in a coffin during the day, and drinking the blood of chickens. But while this might teach you about what it is like for a human to do these things, it doesn't give you information about what it would be like for you to do these things as a vampire.

If there were more research funding available for studies of vampire psychology, scientists might have been able to collect enough experimental data to allow you to make the decision based on whether you had the right personality traits or were the type of person who would be happier as a vampire. You wouldn't be able to use this research to tell you what it would be like to be a vampire, but it would at least tell you approximately how someone like you would report their response to such a change. It would be nice to be able to add in these sorts of facts about empirical results to your deliberations: when you weighed the options from your own perspective you'd want to be able to draw on these results to use them as evidence that contributes to your overall decision.

Of course, unless basically everyone reported being happier as a vampire, to be of any use at all, this research would need to be very fine-grained, given how heterogeneous people are and how different combinations of psychological dispositions and circumstances might radically affect one's response. And, of course, you wouldn't want to make the choice without carefully considering your own personal preferences in addition to the research about people similar to you.[47]

Alas, in the current anti-vampire climate, grants are elusive and no such research has been funded. All you have to go on by way of empirical evidence is what you can observe about how your friends, who are similar to you in some respects, seem to respond to the change.

---

[47] I discuss related issues in the Afterword in the sections on first personal choosing, the fundamental identification problem, and informed consent.

You might not put much stock in what the scientists would come up with even if they had better funding, but you might still think that it was worth paying attention to how your friends and family responded to the experience—and, once they've been bitten, they all think being a vampire is great! But what if it turns out that you aren't just like your friends and family in the relevant respects? You could be a little more sensitive than they are, surely you are a little more sophisticated, and perhaps you are more attuned to the quality of what you eat.

What if it turns out, given your delicate sensibilities, that once you've transformed, you can't *stand* chicken blood—all you'll want to drink is human blood, in particular, the blood of male virgins. (One of your vampire friends confides that he is actually quite finicky now that his palate has been educated about platelet *terroir*.) But contemporary vampire society frowns on drinking human blood, since it isn't good for public relations. And so, if you become a vampire, for the foreseeable future, you'll have to eat food that absolutely disgusts you, and you'll have to constantly confront and overcome your repulsive urge to attack innocent little boys.

The problem here is that you can't predict how your preferences will change. Something that seems disgusting now might seem preferable to the finest of wines once you've been vampirically rewired. Or, you might love the sun right now, and find it impossible to imagine a future without sunbathing. But perhaps, once you've been bitten, you'll remember your days luxuriating on the beach with fondness, but the phenomenal intensity of grasping the true nature of reality as a vampire will simply swamp the value of sunbathing. You'll look back at those days on the beach as pleasant, but also as completely worth giving up for the more intense experiences you are having now. More worryingly, you might now find the idea of being Undead or even the idea of desiring to prefer such a state repulsive and frightening, but once you've been bitten, you might relish it.

Moreover, although everyone you know who has become a vampire tells you how fabulous it is, you might be a little suspicious about their testimony. Maybe they harbor secret regrets, and just want you to be like them. Maybe something about being a vampire warps their views. Or maybe they have no regrets, but are assuming you are just the same as they are in the relevant respects, and so are assuming you will respond just like they did. But what if they are wrong? Why think that just being similar in some rather superficial respects, such as enjoying red wine and liking gothic fiction, or enjoying the same outdoor activities, gives you enough evidence to make such a momentous, irreversible, life-changing choice?

Your effort to evaluate testimony is complicated by the fact that even people who seemed quite anti-vampire beforehand can change their minds after being bitten, suggesting that some sort of deep preference change is indeed occurring. Although your friends, as vampires, report that they are happy with their new existence, it isn't clear that their pre-vampire selves would have been happy with the change. For example, your once-vegetarian neighbor who practiced Buddhism and an esoteric variety of hot yoga now says that since being bitten (as it happens, against her will), she too loves being a vampire.

Maybe something about becoming a vampire changes people in a way so that, *now*, as vampires, they love being vampires. In other words, maybe they engage in a kind of Stockholm syndrome, vampire-style. Or maybe the physical changes involved in turning into a vampire include being hard-wired to love being a vampire when one becomes one. Maybe there are even good evolutionary explanations for why it would be advantageous for vampires to be hard-wired to love being vampires, for, given the inclinations of unenlightened locals equipped with sharp wooden stakes, the species might otherwise dwindle.

This puts you in a dilemma. When you are evaluating testimony, whose testimony should you weight most heavily? The testimony when the person was human? Or their testimony now, when they're a vampire?

In response, you might be inclined to ignore all testimony, attending solely to your own preferences. But then the problems we've already discussed, about what you cannot know before having the experience, will arise. Perhaps you think it's obvious that you shouldn't choose to become a vampire. But what basis do you have for this belief? You don't know what it would be like. On the other hand, perhaps you think it's obvious that you *should* choose to become a vampire. Of course you should choose immortality, superhuman powers and intense new sensory experiences—that sounds great! Again, what basis do you have for your belief? None, it seems. At least, none that is epistemically justified.

What if you pay enough attention to the testimony to think that, even though you aren't inclined to become a vampire because of what you think it might be like, you think you should do it simply because, whatever it will be like to be a vampire, you'll be happy with it once you are one? After all, pretty much everybody says it is great once they become one. But, rationally speaking, this leads back to the problem of which of your preferences you should be most concerned to keep. Which preferences matter more? Your current, human preferences, or the preferences you'd have if you were bitten? How can you rationally choose to ignore your current preferences when making your choice? If you choose to become a vampire simply because you think that the fact of becoming a vampire will make you into a being who will be happy with the choice you've made, you are not choosing by considering the full range of your own (current) preferences.

So how should you choose? If, in the end, you choose to become a vampire based on the exciting possibilities that becoming immortal seems to offer, you shouldn't fool yourself—*you have no idea what you are getting into.* You just don't know what it's like to be a vampire. And if you refuse to become one on the basis that you can't imagine not being human anymore, then you also shouldn't fool yourself—*you have no idea what you are missing.*

The vampire example, and the other examples we've been considering, bring out two problems with our ordinary way of making important personal decisions from our subjective perspective when the decisions involve transformative choices.

First, transformative choices involve epistemically transformative experiences, compromising our ability to rationally assign subjective values to radically new outcomes. The subjective value of the lived experience that is the outcome of choosing to undergo the new experience is epistemically inaccessible to you, and this results in a type of ignorance that standard decision-theoretic models are ill-equipped to handle.

Second, because of the personally transformative nature of the experience, your preferences concerning the acts that lead to the new outcomes can also change. In particular, having the new experience may change your post-experience preferences, or change how your post-experience self values outcomes. Transformative choices, then, ask you to make a decision where you must manage different selves at different times, with different sets of preferences. Which set of preferences should you be most concerned with? Your preferences now, or your preferences after the experience?[48]

And here is the clincher: because of the first problem, you cannot solve the second problem by simply stepping back and choosing by comparing the differences in the subjective values you assign to the outcomes, or by deciding which set of preferences it is somehow better to satisfy. The clincher is that the very same experience is epistemically *and* personally transformative.

The problem doesn't arise in ordinary cases of preference change. In such cases, you can adopt a higher-order approach, where you compare the preferences you'd have before the change to the preferences you'd have after the change, and decide which preferences are the ones you'd prefer to have (and thus the ones that determine how to act). Once you choose your preferred preferences, you can know that you currently prefer to have those preferences, and so you can act in concert with them.[49]

---

[48] I'm indebted to John Collins, Alison Gopnik, Joseph Halpern, Tania Lombrozo, and Richard Pettigrew here, each of whom, independently, encouraged me to make this part of my view more salient to the reader.

[49] Sometimes you don't need to know what it's like in order to make the higher-order decision: you might, for example, simply apply a rule to determine the right result, such as the rule that *it's always better to be smarter*. Applying such a rule might let you rationally choose to avoid taking a drug that would make you stupid but happy. But such a rule must be universal—and it's not even clear that there are such rules. For example, it's not clear *it's always better to be smarter* is

But cases of transformative experience throw a wrench into this procedure. Because you don't know what it will be like to have a transformative experience, you don't know how it will change you, in the sense that you don't know what it will be like to have the new point of view that will determine your new preferences after the experience. More simply: before you have the transformative experience, you can't know what it will be like to be you after the experience. So you can't compare what it's like to be you before the transformative change and what it's like to be you after the change in order to decide which experiential perspective and accompanying set of preferences you'd prefer.[50]

Another way to put the point: If you are to choose rationally, the preferences you have right now seem to have priority, such that to choose rationally you must choose in accordance with the preferences you have now. But your pre-experience information is dramatically incomplete, due to the epistemic inaccessibility of the values of the radically new outcomes. Under such circumstances, why should you be biased towards the preferences of your present self, the epistemically impoverished self? After all, after becoming a vampire you'd know all the values and preferences, and testimony suggests that you'd be deliriously happy, so why shouldn't you choose based on creating, and then satisfying, vampire preferences? If you choose based on your current preferences, you seem to be ignoring information that is important and relevant to your choice. If so, it just isn't clear how you could meet the rational standard when you choose.

This matters. And the reason it matters is that exactly the same problems arise when reasoning about real-life cases. You might have thought that the vampire vignette was fun to think about, but that

---

such a rule. At some point, you could become so smart that you'd be miserable, for everyone around you is insufferably stupid in contrast. The alienation and emotional isolation you'd experience would be profound.

[50] The issues involving decisions that change preferences raise analogous questions for a Bayesian about decisions that change judgments about subjective probabilities.

nothing much turned on it. After all, who cares about an imaginary dilemma where you are considering the obviously amoral, repulsive, and clearly impossible choice to become a vampire? Vampires are so different from us—they aren't even *human*—that the issues such a decision would raise are normally not relevant to practical issues involved in real-world decision-making. You'll never be in a situation where you are choosing to become a vampire, so it doesn't matter that you can't make the decision in any ordinary way. You might have thought that you could safely ignore cases of exotic transformations like becoming a vampire when deliberating about your subjective future and how you want to live your life.

But this misses the point. It is true that the choice to become a vampire is bizarre and otherworldly. The transformation into a vampire would involve a change in species and a change into something that many of us might find morally repulsive, and so is especially strange. But, as the microchip case suggests, transformative decision-making puzzles don't just arise when one is considering an act that transforms a person into another kind of thing altogether. It isn't just choices concerning the fantastic possibility of turning into a vampire, or of turning into a bat, or even of turning into a cat that are transformative. The point of examining the choice of whether to become a vampire is that the structure of transformative choice is reflected in *any* choice that is both epistemically and personally transformative with respect to one's preferences.[51]

In other words, the problems with decision-making involving transformative choices arise for any choice you face that involves having a radically new experience that also substantially changes your personal preferences—and as it turns out, such choices constitute a central part of a normal life. You don't need to consider whether to become a vampire to face this sort of choice—it's just that the possibility of becoming a vampire illustrates the implications of this type

---

[51] I take it as obvious that such choices include ones where the right choice is not determined solely by moral or legal precepts.

of choice especially clearly, by starkly illustrating the decision-making puzzles that come up when you contemplate how to make sense of a decision to become an unknown, dramatically changed, new self.

In any case where you undergo a sufficiently deep personal change, that is, in any case where your core personal preferences are significantly changed, leading to a significant change in how the post-change you would evaluate the act, questions about choices under personal transformation arise. And in any case where you have a truly new kind of experience, such as seeing color for the first time or gaining a new sensory ability, questions about choices under epistemic transformation arise. And for any case where such transformations are combined, and where there is an important role for subjective deliberation and the first personal perspective, the deep questions about the structure and rationality of making transformative choices arise.

In the next chapter, I will argue that some real-life decisions, decisions that are of great personal import, have the structure of transformative decisions. Some of life's biggest choices are choices where we must decide whether to undergo an experience that will change us in ways unknown.

# CHAPTER 3

# LIFE CHOICES

Experiences that are both epistemically and personally transformative create special problems for natural ways we want to deliberate. If we want to rationally choose our acts based on how we envision our possible futures, transformative experiences raise philosophical barriers with practical implications.

When you face a personal decision, you want to be able to consider what it would be like to experience the different possible outcomes of the different alternatives you might choose in order to assess and compare them. But you can't evaluate different possible outcomes involving the lived experience that results from having a transformative experience by attempting to cognitively project forward and consider those possible subjective futures for yourself, because you cannot know what the relevant outcomes are like until you've actually experienced them. In other words, you have to have the transformative experience itself before you can know the expected subjective value of the act that concerns it. If your decision is momentous and leads to irreversible consequences, then you face a deep and serious problem—how are you supposed to make your choice?

There are many epistemically and personally transformative big decisions made in real life that fit this structure.[1] For example, consider a recruit's choice about whether to enlist. If the recruit has no

---

[1] Olympic swimmer Ian Thorpe (2012) has described what it's like to win a gold medal—and also to defend a gold—as being an experience that you couldn't understand until you experienced it.

experience of war, what it is like to be on the front lines of a battle can be a transformative experience, as the evidence of post-traumatic shock amongst veterans can testify to.[2] If such an experience is transformative, as it likely is, and on the assumption that there is reasonable variation amongst the experiences of new recruits (some experience a newfound sense of glory and heroism, some experience fear, and so on), a new recruit who is likely to go to the front lines if he enlists cannot make a rational choice about whether to enlist based on his subjective projections for the future. I am assuming that the choice is not simply forced, and that it is not based solely on third personal factors like the objective value of performing one's patriotic duties.

So how should the possible recruit decide whether to enlist? He has no idea about what it will really be like on the front lines, so what can he use to make his choice in a rationally justified way?

Maybe he should assume that it is always, or almost always, a terrifically bad experience to be on the front lines. Maybe the recruit would decline to enlist for this reason, or perhaps sign up for purely unselfish reasons, love for one's country swamping any personal expectations.

Now, I think such assumptions are simplistic: unless the country is under direct attack, personal expectations usually play a significant role in deciding whether to enlist. And assuming that being on the front lines must be a bad experience is also simplistic, in part because the fact that a situation involves suffering and fear does not entail that it is, all things considered, an experience with a negative value. There is subjective value in life experience, and subjective value in heroism, and subjective value in sacrificing your comfort and happiness for the sake of your country. But if you can assume (and I admit this is not without justification!)

---

[2] For those of us who haven't experienced it, stories and films might at least help us see that there must be much we can't grasp about the nature and intensity of such an experience, e.g. the storming of Omaha Beach in the opening scenes of *Saving Private Ryan*. Also see Keegan (1976) and Fussell (1989) for eye-opening discussions of the horrific experiences of individual soldiers.

that the negative value of the experience of being on the front lines is very likely to outweigh the positive value of all these other experiences, although you can't actually know what it is like to be on the front lines at wartime, you can rationally choose to avoid it on this basis.[3]

The point here, as I noted in chapter 2, is that some transformative choices don't need to be made based on knowledge about future experience. The outcomes of some acts do not need to be assessed by modeling yourself in future situations when there is no need to try to discover the values of the outcomes in this way. If you have evidence that every relevant experiential outcome would be a bad experience for you, and that your preferences would remain constant through the experience, then you have a good reason to assign all of them a negative subjective value without trying to determine the values by assessing how you, personally, would experience the outcomes. For example, consider a decision to step in front of an oncoming train. All of the relevant outcomes involve death or significant injury. Even if you don't know what it would be like to experience those injuries or to experience dying from them (and of course, death entails the end of experience), it is rational for you to avoid stepping in front of the train.

In cases where everyone's well-being, or almost everyone's well-being, is reduced (or improved) by making a particular choice to do something, and everyone or almost everyone recognizes and agrees with this assessment of the change in well-being, and everyone's preferences remain constant, then you will not need to rely on personal reflection to assess a decision. In this sort of case, we usually prefer to just decide by the numbers—because engaging in reflective deliberation to imaginatively assess which of the different possible outcomes would be better or worse is pointless. If an outcome is bad for everyone, then it is bad for the decision-maker. It's only when there is a range of possible subjective values from good to bad for the outcomes that she will be faced with a subjective decision procedure that requires

---

[3] Keegan (1976); and Fussell (1989).

the ability to assign values to outcomes and determine her preferences based on knowing what the experience will be like.

So while some kinds of decisions obviously don't require cognitive modeling, others do. Even assessments of outcomes for mundane, everyday decisions often rely on cognitive modeling. When you consider where you'd like to go for vacation, it is natural to decide between possible locales by imagining yourself in different situations in order to assess your preferences for walking on the beach versus cross-country skiing versus visiting the Louvre. When you buy a house, it is natural to imagine yourself living in the different possible homes you are considering in order to choose which one you'd prefer to live in. Simulating ourselves in different situations is a decision-making tool we use to help us to make decisions when general considerations are insufficient to determine the expected value of an act. Sometimes the personal simulation is necessary when the general constraints are insufficiently restrictive, and sometimes it is necessary when the constraints are insufficiently fine-grained, that is, when knowing how you'd value an outcome depends on knowing your individual psychological response to a situation.

Choices involving familiar outcomes, like houses you've seen or places you've visited, do not present a problem when we need to cognitively model in order to assess the expected value of an act. But transformative choices involving radically new experiences do, because they involve epistemically inaccessible subjective values and preference changes. Consider the choice of whether to engage in an uprising that is part of a democratic revolution. You don't know what such an upheaval could bring, especially if your country has been politically stable until now, and at least one possible outcome of the revolution could be the installment of a new regime that is even more oppressive. In such a case, you may want to participate because you think that the people oppressed by the current regime, you and others like you, will live a better life under the new regime. But since you do not have enough information to construct and assess your responses to different possible outcomes, and since the experience of political upheaval can be transformative, you cannot use your simulations of what it would be like after the revolution as evidence for a decision about whether to participate.

Or consider a decision to have radical surgery to remove a malignant tumor. The surgery will result in permanent pain, disability, and disfigurement, yet if you don't have it you are likely to die from the tumor. You don't know what life could be like after the surgery, although you know it will be painful, but you don't know what it is like to die, either. You must choose between receiving the treatment and extending your life, or almost certainly going into hospice care and having a shorter, but less painful life. Such a choice is deeply frightening, partly because all of the possible outcomes are bad, and partly because you don't know how to evaluate your options to make the choice that best respects the preferences of your future self.

## Sensory Abilities

A different sort of case involves dramatic sensory changes in individuals with disabilities. These experiences have the potential to vary widely with regard to the subjective values of the outcomes, and so assumptions about the overwhelming likelihood of an experiential outcome being obviously good or obviously bad can be unjustified.[4] The sorts of decisions that have the structure of transformative choices involve decisions about devices that can endow their recipients with new sensory abilities, such as cochlear implants or retinal surgery. (Retinal transplants may soon become possible.)

Consider a profoundly deaf person, someone who has been deaf from birth, who must decide whether her profoundly deaf child, who has also been deaf from birth, should receive a cochlear implant.[5]

---

[4]  See Carel (2014b); and Barnes (2016).

[5]  I will assume, for simplicity, that we are addressing the decision of implantation in terms of a single cochlear implant, although bilateral implantation is also an option.

Cochlear implants do not magnify sounds like a hearing aid does. Instead, they directly stimulate the auditory nerve. Signals generated by the implant are then processed by the brain as sound.[6]

Cochlear implants can give people with profound and severe hearing loss a new kind of sensory experience: they gain access to a wide variety of sounds, including access to spoken language and to auditory properties of the environment. Ideally, from the medical perspective, the device is implanted when the child is very young, in order to provide the best development of spoken language and to give access to sounds while the child is developing both physically and cognitively. Thus, in the normal case, the parents of a deaf child should decide whether or not to implant the device during the child's first year of life. While such implants have been steadily gaining in popularity, and are now the dominant choice for parents with a hearing-impaired child, there has been significant controversy over their use. The controversy stemmed partly from the fact that, while large medical corporations, experts in the medical community, mainstream media, and some members of the hearing population strongly supported the use of cochlear implants, especially in children, many members of the Deaf[7] community resisted mass implantation.[8]

To understand this opposition, it is important to realize that over many years, the Deaf community has built a strong and distinctive social structure designed to provide support and inclusion for

---

[6] For a brief overview of the technology and its applications, see NIDCD (2014).

[7] The capitalization of "Deaf" indicates reference to or membership in the Deaf community and culture, while "deaf" is a biological or merely physical term used to describe a person with significant hearing impairment. See Harman (2009) for an interesting discussion of the moral questions and political controversy surrounding the decision to give a deaf child a cochlear implant and a different way of framing the debate over cochlear implants and preferences.

[8] In one much-discussed case, a Deaf couple deliberately selected to have a deaf child (Spriggs 2002).

a group of people, the physically deaf, who were historically discriminated against and excluded from mainstream society. The use of signed languages and other alternative means to communicate contributed to the development of a unique Deaf culture, with its own distinctive approach to the arts and other forms of expression. From the Deaf community's perspective, Deaf culture is just one among many intrinsically valuable world cultures, on a par with traditional cultures, and provides its members with shared experiences and support that is unavailable in any other way. Deaf culture thus makes its own rich and unique contribution to the cultural panorama given by a wide view of human civilization. To fully belong to the Deaf community, a person must identify primarily as Deaf and must identify with Deaf culture, must use a signed language, and arguably must even have a signed language as his or her first or primary language.[9]

Advocates for the Deaf community have argued that there are intensely negative values for deaf infants who receive cochlear implants, since they never have the opportunity to have the special, extensive, and uniquely shared experiences of being a deaf member of a Deaf community, and they also miss out on many other rich experiences tied to not hearing sounds, experiences that a species-typical hearing person does not and cannot have. Peter Artinian, a profoundly deaf parent of three deaf children, eloquently describes his view:

> But for myself, I'm deaf forever. I like it quiet. I like it peaceful…You know, I see that, you know—I see other people getting all agitated by the sounds around them. But me, I just sort of, you know, it rolls off my back because it's quiet and I'm comfortable there.[10]

Some even suggest that using a signed language "may determine, or at least modify, the thought processes of those who sign, and give

---

[9] A parallel is sometimes drawn with being black and participating in Black culture.

[10] Peter Artinian, *Talk of the Nation* (2006).

them a unique and untranslatable, hypervisual cognitive style" and "that [a deaf child] constructs her world in a different way, perhaps radically so."[11] In other words, being deaf (and Deaf) gives one a distinct, unique cognitive experience.[12] The distinctive poetry and other art generated by the Deaf community supports this suggestion, and the National Association of the Deaf is clear about its mandate for the protection of the Deaf experience.

Participating in this unique and valuable community and culture gives a deaf person a unique, intrinsically valuable Deaf experience and fosters a community that provides support for a historically oppressed segment of society. This is the ground for the importance that members of the Deaf community assign to being part of it. The intense push for cochlear implants from members of the medical community, backed by the pharmaceutical companies that produced and marketed the device, was regarded by many Deaf people as no less than an attempt by members of hearing communities, bolstered by powerful political and business interests, to obliterate the distinctive Deaf culture and its contributions and to assimilate those who were implanted into hearing society as second-class, "disabled," or once-disabled members. Activist members of the Deaf community responded to this pressure by resisting cochlear implants and the idea that deafness is a disability or illness that needs to be "cured," arguing that the experiences of being Deaf and participating in Deaf culture are rich and positive ones that need to be given more weight in the decision procedure, and many Deaf parents refused to have the devices implanted in their young children.

Many of those who reject the implants say they do so because they believe the value of being a deaf member of the Deaf community outweighs the value of being able to hear via a cochlear implant. Part of this skepticism is sometimes tied to facts

[11] Sacks (1991, p. 74).
[12] See also Blankmeyer Burke (2014).

about the technology: while the devices are improving, cochlear implants do not yet provide hearing at the level of those who were never deaf, and Deaf people argue that being a fully accepted member of the Deaf community is infinitely preferable to being a partial hearer who cannot be fully integrated into the hearing community.

Also relevant is the fact that the experience of those who are deaf from birth and then receive the cochlear implant is held to be different from the experience of those who, perhaps because of hearing loss later in life, receive the implant after having heard sounds, since memory and other cognitive functions play a significant role in the functioning of the implant. Moreover, cochlear implants do not allow people to hear in the same way as those who hear naturally. A final concern involves the parent–child bond. Both hearing parents and Deaf parents want to have a deep and meaningful connection to and communication with their child. Hearing parents often want their child to be implanted in order to foster connection and communication.

Deaf parents sometimes resist the implant for the very same reason. They want their children to be members of the same community as they are, and may want to share the deep and personal experience of being Deaf as part of the familial bond. If a child of Deaf parents receives a cochlear implant, she may find herself isolated from her closest family members and those who are best able to provide loving support and guidance throughout her childhood and young adulthood. While there are many different reasons why the decision is fraught for parents, at least some of the central worries concern the nature of the future experiences of the child, including how the changes to the child's capacities will affect the parent–child relationship.

Advocates for the implants argue that having the ability bestowed by the implants to hear sounds is of great positive value, implicitly arguing that it is so great that it outweighs the values defended by members of the Deaf community.[13] The claim is that the relative values are reversed: the value of being able to hear sounds and thus become a functioning member of the hearing community via a cochlear implant, even if the hearing is different from normal hearing, is so high that it outweighs the values and preferences of the Deaf advocate who is opposed to implantation.

So there is an impasse, with each side claiming that its values and preferences must be respected. The situation is complicated by the fact that, in most cases where a cochlear implant is being considered, the parents are making the decision about the implant for their young child, not for themselves, and implantation can be irreversible. Since both implantation and removal can cause significant damage to the physical structure and auditory capacities of the inner ear, surgery may reduce or even eliminate any remaining capacity to hear naturally in the implanted ear.

What I want to bring out is the way that each of these decisions about a cochlear implant, the one made by the Deaf parents and the one made by the hearing parents, involve an epistemically transformative element as well as a personally transformative element. My objective is to show that there is another dimension to this debate that is worth exploring.

The structure of this case is, in some ways, like the case we considered in chapter 2, where we have to decide whether we want to replace our capacity to taste with an unknown sensory ability. In many cases where the child has profound hearing loss, Deaf parents of the child need to decide whether their deaf child should receive an implant, or parents who have had their hearing from birth need to decide whether their deaf child should receive an implant. An important argument that advocates for the cochlear implant may

[13] Neil Levy (2002, p. 153) discusses these issues in detail, concluding, "Though Deaf culture might well be intrinsically valuable, I conclude—with regret—that the kinds of measures that would be required to maintain it are not permissible."

make is that the child's subjective future, that is, what it will be like to be her, or what her future lived experience will be like, will be better if she receives the implant. That is, they could argue that the subjective value of her future experiences will be higher if she receives the implant than if she does not. Those who argue against the implant could argue for the opposite conclusion—that the subjective value of her future experiences will be higher if she does not receive the implant.

My suggestion is that understanding the transformative nature of the experience involved, and the implications this can have for one's ability to rationally evaluate the possible outcomes for the child, adds a new dimension to the way we should think about this issue.

In particular, shedding light on the transformative nature of the choice can allow us to cast doubt on how parents can be expected to rationally evaluate these arguments about the subjective value of future experience, for such arguments may implicitly require parents to ascribe values to experiences and to assess preference changes that they lack epistemic access to. Given the epistemic inaccessibility of what it is like to be Deaf from a hearing person's point of view, a parent who is a member of the hearing community who has never been Deaf cannot know enough about what it is like to be a deaf member of the Deaf community to assign a subjective value to the child's possible future experiences as a deaf person, and by extension to the subjective value of the child's future experiences as a deaf member of the Deaf community. If the experience of being a Deaf member of the Deaf community is unique, a person who is not Deaf, especially one who is not a deaf member of the Deaf community, cannot know what it is like to have this kind of Deaf experience, and thus cannot assign a subjective value to the experience based on what she thinks it is like, or assess the experience-based preferences of a deaf person who is Deaf.[14]

---

[14] A hearing person may be able to assign a value to being a hearing member of the Deaf community if she correctly identifies with the community.

But the inaccessibility is perfectly parallel on the other side. A Deaf parent who has never been able to hear or does not have "species-typical hearing" cannot know what it is like to be a species-typical hearing member of a hearing community. This means she cannot assign a subjective value to the child's possible future experiences as a species-typical hearing person, and she cannot use her experiential knowledge to determine and compare (what she cognitively projects will be) the deaf child's preferences, should she remain deaf, with the child's preferences as a hearing person.[15] The case of the Deaf experience is a real-life version of the case of ordinary Mary: those that are deaf since birth and those that have been hearers since birth are like ordinary Mary in her black-and-white room. In just the same way that, before she leaves her room, Mary cannot know what it is like to see color or know how her preferences will evolve when she has the transformative experience of seeing color, there is something the parents of the deaf child cannot know, because they have not had the necessary experience.

If a hearing parent can't assign a subjective value to the relevant kind of Deaf experience, then that outcome's value is epistemically inaccessible to her, and she cannot rationally compare it to the subjective value of the hearing experience. Moreover, if she does not know what it is like to have the Deaf experience, she cannot calculate or compare preferences based on what it is like to be Deaf to preferences based on what it is like to be a hearer.

If a Deaf parent can't assign a value to the (relevant) hearing experience of a member of the hearing community, then that outcome's value is epistemically inaccessible to her, and she cannot rationally compare it to the subjective value of the Deaf experience. Moreover, because she lacks the requisite experiential knowledge, she cannot determine or assess what the deaf child's new values and preferences would be, were she to become a hearer. If the child receives the implant and has the transformative experience of becoming a hearing

---

[15] This holds whether or not the implant bestows sufficiently complete hearing abilities.

person in a hearing community, this will change her preferences in ways that a Deaf parent who has never had species-typical hearing cannot cognitively represent or model. This means that, just like the hearing parent, the Deaf parent cannot compare preferences for the different possible acts.

The decision to implant is complicated by the very strong cultural and legal presumption that it should be the parents, not the medical experts, who determine whether the child is implanted. When the parents make this difficult decision, they are supposed to make this determination by considering the empirical data about the success and problems of such implants for other children, but they are also supposed to weigh the data in light of their personal judgments about the future subjective well-being and lived experience of their child.[16]

In general,

> As decisionmakers for children, parents are expected to weigh all relevant factors such as the risks, benefits, alternatives of treatment, a particular child's pain tolerance, her medical, and social history, and proceed in accordance with whatever course is, all things considered, in the child's best interests. Deciding whether a particular course of treatment or non-treatment is in an individual child's best interests requires an assessment of the relative importance of each factor. Clinicians and ethicists who place primary emphasis on the principle of respect for autonomy tend to conceive the assessment as a subjective one belonging to the parent, who is free to consider religious, familial, or other values in assessing treatment options. In other words, the commitment to autonomy is expressed through value neutrality—an obligation not to interfere with the choice of another—regardless of whether the decisionmaker is the principal or a surrogate. Except in the rare circumstance in which the decision will have devastating consequences for the child, the commitment to autonomy requires deference to parental choice. Parents, after all, are in the

---

[16] Some of those in the bioethics community argue that we must assume disability is a harmful condition. See, for example, Savulescu and Kahane (2009). As I have argued, I think the assumption that being a typical hearer is preferable to being Deaf is epistemically unwarranted.

best position to know what is best for a child. Clinicians and ethicists will thus presume their choices to be in the best interests of the child.

> The commitment to parental autonomy expressed through value neutrality is evident in many legal cases in which courts have refused to second guess parental choices about a child's medical care despite medical recommendations for a different course of action.[17]

So the decision procedure cannot simply be transformed into a decision based solely on third personal facts about the success or failure of cochlear implants without serious changes in the established norms surrounding such decisions. In the usual case, then, it is the parents who should make the decision about whether their young child should receive the implant, and they are expected to do it while considering expert advice and data, but ultimately by *relying on their own subjective evaluation of the situation.*

The importance of the first personal perspective is, in fact, embedded in the way many people value informed consent. As a patient, I am the one who must make the decision about what happens to my body and what care I want to receive, to determine what is best for me. On some accounts, I'm supposed to do this by considering the relevant costs and benefits of choosing each act, weighing the possible outcomes in light of my own views about how I want my future to be and what risks I'm prepared to take, given the ways that my life might be better if I choose that particular option. I don't just use the probabilities about states and values of outcomes reported from the testimony of others to decide the question.[18] This is just a version of the discussion we had in the first chapter, when we considered the imaginary but evocative decision of whether to become a vampire.

The parallel exists for both the epistemic and the personal elements of transformation involved in the decision. The

---

[17] Ouellette (2011, p. 1263).

[18] There is debate about the right way to think about informed consent. For an interesting and thoughtful discussion, see Kukla's (2005).

transformative choice involved in getting a cochlear implant asks parents to choose between acts leading to very different possible futures for their child, where each possible future represents their child as a person with very different experiences and core personal preferences.

When facing the decision to implant, the Deaf parent doesn't know how the implantation will change her child, in the sense that she doesn't know what it will be like to have the hearing experiences and new preferences that the child will have after receiving a cochlear implant. The hearing parent doesn't know how it will change her child, in the sense that she doesn't know what it would have been like to have the Deaf experiences and preferences that the child would have had if she did not receive a cochlear implant. This means that neither type of parent can compare what it would be like for that child to grow up with an implant with what it would be like for that child to grow up without an implant in order to decide which experiential perspective and accompanying set of preferences should be preferred. Should the values, experiences, and preferences of a Deaf person be preferred? Or should the values, experiences, and preferences of a hearing person be preferred? Should the Deaf parent make the choice consistent with her own preferences regarding the Deaf experience, or is she somehow expected to take into account the preferences that her child would have as a hearing person? Should the hearing parent make the choice consistent with her own preferences regarding the hearing experience, or is she somehow expected to take into account the preferences that her child would have as a Deaf person?

The importance we assign to making decisions like these from our subjective point of view brings out a new dimension in which parents of deaf children can be seen as caught in a deep and difficult decision-making quandary. If the decision to implant the device is based in any significant way on the expectation that the parent is to compare the subjective values and preferences involved in different

possible future lived experiences of the child, there can be no normative guide for rational action in this case. For if the parent is expected
to take into account values and preferences that are epistemically
inaccessible to her, it is unclear how such a choice is to be rationally
justified. And if there is any choice that a person wants to be able to
make rationally, so as to result in the best possible outcome, it would
be a choice that fundamentally affected the nature and character of
her child's future.

My arguments are intended to bring out how this debate may
be complicated in ways that have not been explicitly or fully recognized. (I am not arguing that the debate has actually developed
along these lines.) The fact that transformative decision-making is
involved means that the issue has a purely epistemic dimension, one
derived from deep and far-reaching facts about the limitations of the
human mind. This isn't just a case where we are comparing the social
value of Deaf culture to the personal rights of a child. And it isn't a
case where the side that gets to make the decision, for example, the
side of the Deaf parents, has to be convinced or forced to "make the
right decision."

My arguments suggest that our understanding of the debate over
cochlear implants can be developed in new ways. There is more to
the issue than whether we should assign priority to the physical
ability to hear sounds over membership in a unique and intrinsically
valuable culture.[19] The debate can also be understood as involving
questions about whether one of the most natural ways to frame the
issue, as a choice between different acts that will determine how
one's child experiences his or her subjective future, is a framing that
prevents the parent from proceeding rationally. In other words, our
natural inclination to want to make the choice by projecting forward into the imagined future lived experience of the child under
each possibility, the possibility of being a deaf member of the Deaf
community and the possibility of becoming a hearing member of

[19] Levy (2002).

the hearing community, does not give us a decision structure that allows for a rational choice.[20]

My discussion of cochlear implants has implications for other debates over differences in abilities based on different phenomenological capacities. The issue is even more pressing than one might realize given recent work in cognitive neuroscience, for example, work which shows how seemingly different sensory modalities are actually intertwined.

In other words, adding a new sensory capacity always comes with some sort of tradeoff, often a sensory tradeoff, and certainly with significant changes and tradeoffs with respect to other features of one's cognitive phenomenology. For example, experiences of seeing and hearing are not entirely separate, because the sensory processing of them is not separate. Eye movements affect the sounds a person hears, because the brain combines stimuli from eye movements, among other things, including auditory stimuli, to construct the sounds we hear (or, in other words, to construct the representation of sound that we experience).[21]

Correspondence between the visual and auditory scenes is governed by eye position relative to the head, and the brain does not build total experience by simply adding together separate sensory experiences. Our cognitive response to the external world does not work by engaging in distinct processes responding to entirely separate external stimuli to generate independent sensory experiences that the perceiver simply adds together. Rather, different

[20] As a matter of fact, cochlear implants are gaining in popularity. The likely reason for the success of the movement to implant cochlear devices is the fact that most children who are born with or develop profound hearing loss have parents who have been hearers from birth. These parents are far more inclined to decide in favor of cochlear implants, and so the number of adults who are deaf from birth or from early childhood is diminishing. But the fact that most people choose cochlear implants doesn't make it the right choice. And it certainly doesn't make it a rational choice.

[21] The McGurk effect is a familiar example of this.

types of stimuli are combined and interpreted to generate a holistic conscious experience. For example, if someone hears and sees normally, her brain doesn't work by simply processing auditory stimuli into hearing and visual stimuli into seeing. Instead, visual and auditory stimuli are processed and interpreted together to create the person's experience of hearing. This implies, among other things, that because their eye movements are not tied to visual images, blind people experience sounds differently from those who can see.

This brings out how there can be a deep experiential difference between those who have a particular sensory capacity and those who do not. You can't know what it's like to be blind simply by closing your eyes.[22] You can't know what it's like to be deaf (or Deaf) simply by stopping up your ears. The holistic nature of the construction of experience means that differences in experience between those with different sensory capacities are differences *in kind*.

Empirically, there is no question that at the most basic conscious level, the first personal experience of the congenitally blind or congenitally deaf is deeply different in kind from first personal experience of sighted and hearing individuals. The difference in first personal experience between the blind and the sighted is evident from the centrality of vision in the cognitive development of sighted children.

---

[22] It is unclear whether a person who has been blind from birth could hear in the same way as someone who is sighted or who was once sighted. Given the role of visual stimuli in the construction of sound, the sighted and the blind use different stimuli to construct auditory experience, with sighted people relying heavily on visual cues, and the blind relying heavily on echolocation and other auditory and kinesthetic cues, and this suggests that the phenomenal character of what is heard by a sighted person will be different from the phenomenal character of what is heard by a blind person. And given the role of previous stimuli in how the brain "learns" to interpret and process stimuli, those who have never been sighted may be permanently physically different from those who are or have been sighted in how they produce sound experience. Similar points apply to deaf people and those with cochlear implants. I'm indebted to discussions with Jennifer Groh here.

Children learn about the world through sensations such as seeing shapes, feeling softness, and listening to sounds...Unlike sighted children, blind children do not see colours or faces, they do not follow the gaze of others, they do not see mountains, elephants, or a flickering fire, and the fact that two people are hugging near by is largely inaccessible to them. Blind infants have limited opportunities to observe objects, actions, and the perceptual states of other people. They have no access to facial expressions or eye gaze, and do not share first-person experiences of seeing with the sighted people around them.[23]

Understanding what it is like to be blind, if you are not yourself blind, is not just a matter of imaginatively subtracting away what it is like to see from the rest of your experience. Understanding what it is like to be deaf, if you are not yourself deaf, is not just a matter of imaginatively subtracting away what it is like to hear from the rest of your experience. Differences in the kinds of experiences we have, in addition to being drawn from the cultural and intellectual experiences of the individual, are also drawn from purely phenomenal differences in the kinds of experiences involved, given the preconscious and holistic construction of experience from external stimuli. If this is the case, then our ability to imagine losing a dominant sensory ability may be as limited as our ability to imagine having a new sensory ability.

So although the example from chapter 2, of trading one's sense of taste for an entirely new sense modality, was fictional, it models real-life epistemic possibilities with transformative decisions. Such possibilities could include a decision faced by someone who is considering physical enhancement,[24] a decision faced by a blind person considering surgery to become sighted, or a decision faced by a Deaf person considering surgery to become a hearer.[25]

---

[23] Bedny and Saxe (2012, p. 57).

[24] See Agar (2010).

[25] In the Afterword, I explore a way that hierarchical Bayesian modeling could be used to develop partial models for decisions about changes in one's sensory capacities, using an example involving congenital blindness.

## Choosing to Have a Child

Cases involving our capacity to see or to hear have obvious connections to the example of ordinary Mary we discussed in chapter 2. But there are other types of big decisions that involve transformative choices. Consider the decision to have a child.[26] This is a decision, at least as it is characterized in many contemporary societies, that you are supposed to approach by deliberating about whether you want to become a parent, all things considered.

So imagine the following scenario. You have no children. However, you have reached a point in your life when you might be ready to have a child. You discuss it with your partner and contemplate your options, reflecting on the choice and its outcomes by envisioning what it would be like for you to have a child of your very own and comparing this to what you think it would be like to remain childless. After careful consideration, you make your decision.

In chapter 2, I described this sort of deliberation in terms of cognitive modeling: it's very natural to try to represent what it would be like to have a child by imagining or simulating the outcome of having a child. And then perhaps you imaginatively represent the outcome of what it's like to remain childless in order to assess what it would be like to live your life unencumbered. Many use a procedure like this when they decide to have a child. Many use it when they decide to remain childless.

In the scenario described above, the way you make your choice follows cultural norms where couples are encouraged to think carefully and clearly about what they want their future lives to be like before deciding to start a family. Many prospective parents decide to have a baby because they have a deep desire to have children, based on the (perhaps inarticulate) sense that the lived experience of being a parent will make their lives fuller, happier, and more meaningful. The

---

[26] "Some of the material in this section was drawn from my (2015a) "What you can't expect when you're expecting," *Res Philosophica*.

process of envisioning what it would be like to have a child in order to help you make this decision is not just something that wealthy and middle-class parents do. There is evidence that many poor women, including very young mothers contemplating a child out of wedlock, also see having a child as a chief source of identity and meaning, and that these women also deliberate by envisioning themselves as mothers. "Thoughts of children—when to have them, who with, what they'll be like—often preoccupy the hopes and dreams."[27] Women may also envision having a closer relationship with the prospective father, and think having a child is a good route to that outcome.

Of course, there are many other situations where you might find yourself in the situation of choosing to have a child. Perhaps the pregnancy was unplanned, but now that you find yourself pregnant, you have to choose whether to continue the pregnancy.[28] When you deliberate in this situation, a natural and ordinary part of the deliberation involves reflecting on what you think it would be like for you to have this child and whether you are ready for what this entails, and comparing this to what you think it would be like to remain childless.

In this section, I will focus my discussion on the experience of physically producing an infant, its immediate aftermath, and the extended experience of raising this child from infancy to adulthood.

---

[27] Edin and Kefalas (2007, p. 32). Why do so many poor, very young women have a child early, instead of deciding to terminate the pregnancy in order to wait until they are older, financially more stable, and married? "The key to the mystery…lies in what they hope their children will do for them" (p. 10). Often, for poor men and women, a child is an accomplishment, and is seen as an emotional and physical way to connect. "In the woman's view, the birth of a baby ought to transform the father into a family man who is as selflessly devoted to the well-being of the child as she is, just as it has transformed her" (p. 102).

[28] I am assuming, first, that terminating the pregnancy is an option, and second, that you have not automatically ruled this option out for moral or religious reasons. Obviously, in addition to considerations about your own future, the deliberation often includes consideration of the (possible) child's future, and of the moral, religious, and other non-subjective questions involved.

Of course, one can choose to become a parent without physically producing one's child, for example, by adopting a child. I'll discuss the experience of being a parent without physically producing the child in the next section.

When deliberating about the choice to have one's first child, prospective parents reflect on how they want their lives to go and what kind of person they take themselves to be. Guides for prospective parents often suggest that people ask themselves if having a baby will enhance an already happy life, and encourage prospective parents to reflect on, for example, how they see themselves in five and ten years' time, whether they feel ready to care for and nurture the human being they want to create, whether they think they'd be a happy and content mother (or father), whether having a baby of their very own would make life more meaningful, whether they are ready for the tradeoffs that come with being a parent, whether they desire to continue with their current career plans or other personal projects, and so on.

Some people want to have a child because they believe a baby will fill their lives with love, or because they want to be loved and needed by another person. Some take motherhood to be a supremely fulfilling vocation.[29] But others see liberation in the decision to avoid parenthood. They reject presumptions that equate child-rearing with happiness or self-realization, and object to those who look with pity or suspicion on the happily childfree. Insofar as there is any consensus, it's around the idea that you, as the prospective parent, should reflect with great care on these issues and decide whether this sort of life is for you.

Of course, many people recognize that the choice has important implications that extend past their own concerns. But the decision is

---

[29] This may or may not be the same as increasing one's "life satisfaction" or "meaningfulness." Also, I am ignoring external, nonphenomenal factors one might weigh when making a choice about whether to procreate, such as the objective values of environmental impact or population control. A version of my argument that takes these factors into account holds unless these values are supposed to swamp the personal subjective values.

thought to necessarily involve an intimate, personal component, and as such, it is a decision best made from the standpoints of prospective parents. Since (in the usual case) the parents assume primary responsibility for the child they create, it seems appropriate to frame the decision in terms of making a personal choice that carefully weighs the values of one's possible future experiences, especially given the contemporary emphasis on one's personal responsibility for one's own children. So it isn't that other, nonsubjective values don't matter, but when it comes to your own life and the possibility of producing a child, your subjective values and preferences concerning the sorts of responsibilities you are willing to take on, the tradeoffs and sacrifices you are willing to make, and other features of how you regard the lived experience of being a parent need to play a central role in the deliberation.[30]

Speaking in decision-theoretic terms, you are deciding whether to have a child based on the expected value of the act for you and your partner. You are to think about what it would be like to have a child, how it will change you and your partner, and how it will influence the other parts of your life, so that you can assess the subjective values of the relevant outcomes. Even if the contemplation is not as detailed or precise as the perfect rational agent could make it, an approximation of this approach embodies our ordinary way of trying to take an authentic, clear-headed, careful, and normatively rational approach to this extremely important decision.

When deliberating in this case, the choice is between having one's own child or not having one's own child. For the act of having your child, the relevant outcomes are the experiences of what it is like for you to have a child, including what it is like to have the beliefs, desires, emotions, and dispositions that result, directly and indirectly, from having your own child, and the relevant subjective values are determined by these experiences. For the act of remaining childless, the relevant outcomes have subjective values determined by what it is like for you to

---

[30] See Brase and Brase (2012) for interesting work exploring the psychological reasons behind "baby fever."

live a childfree life. Not having a child means that you'll have very different experiences from ones you'll have if you do have a child, and has follow-on effects, such as the fact that, other things being equal, you'll have significantly more sleep and significantly fewer financial costs if you remain childless. Framing the decision this way is neither surprising nor unusual from a commonsensical point of view.

Of course, having a child or not having a child will have value with respect to plenty of other things, such as the local demographic and the environment. However, the primary focus here is on an agent who is trying to decide, largely independently of these external or impersonal factors, whether she wants to have a child of her own. In this case, the subjective values of the experiences stemming from the choice about having a child play the central role in the decision to procreate.

The subjective values of experiential outcomes are still relevant even if we take a wider scope for values, since even in cases with a wider purview, the subjective value of what it is like for the agent to have her own child must be evaluated in order to determine the expected value of her choice. For instance, you might choose to have a child because you desire to have some of your DNA transmitted to future generations. But the value of satisfying this desire must be weighed against the subjective value of other outcomes. If, as is likely, the subjective value of what it is like for you to have your own child is sufficiently positive or sufficiently negative, it could swamp the value of satisfying your desire to leave a genetic imprint.

When choosing, as always, we want to try to meet the normative standard. To choose rationally, you determine the approximate value of each relevant outcome, you determine the weighted value of each outcome given the probability of the world being such that the relevant state would occur, and then use this information to estimate the expected value of each act, choosing the act with the highest expected value.

So, in this scenario, when you deliberate about whether to have your first child, to do it rationally, you are supposed to (at least approximately) assess your subjective values for the outcomes stemming from choosing to have a child or choosing to remain childless, determine any relevant probabilities, identify the act that maximizes your expected subjective value, and then act in accordance with your preferences, that is, choose the act with the highest expected subjective value. The problem, however, is that if you try to approach the question this way, you find yourself with a decision that has the structure of a transformative choice.

Why? Because before a person has had a child, she is in an epistemic situation like that of ordinary Mary before she leaves her black-and-white room. Recall that when Mary chooses to leave her black-and-white room to see color for the first time, she undergoes an epistemically transformative experience: she learns something she could not have known before leaving her room. What she learns, when she leaves her room and sees red for the first time, is something she could only learn from experience—what it's like to see red.

Because of her limited experience and information, before Mary leaves her room, she faces a deep subjective unpredictability about the future. Not only does Mary not know what it'll be like to see red before she sees it, she also doesn't know what emotions, beliefs, desires, and dispositions will be caused by what it's like for her to see red. Maybe she'll feel joy and elation. Or maybe she'll feel fear and despair. And so on. And all of these new emotions, whatever they are, will change her preferences about seeing color. Maybe red will become her favorite color. Or maybe she'll run back to her room and refuse to leave it ever again. She doesn't know, and so she cannot predict, the subjective values of the experiential outcomes of her act, and she doesn't know how her preferences will change as the result of that experience.

Before she has her first child, a prospective parent is in the same sort of situation. Just like Mary, who doesn't know what it's like to see color before she leaves her black-and-white room, the prospective parent, until she actually has her child, doesn't know what it's like to have a child of her very own.

How can this be? After all, there are many books devoted to telling pregnant women and their partners what to expect. Parents and prospective grandparents regale them with stories. Birthing classes are offered at the local hospital.

But descriptions, testimony, and practicing deep breathing won't help—they are no more effective at teaching you what it's like to actually experience having your own child than descriptions designed to teach Mary about what it's like for her to see red.[31] Even experience with other children won't teach you what it's like to have your own: prospective parents can have nieces and nephews, change diapers and babysit, and have much younger siblings they care for. But, as many parents know, you feel differently about your own child.

While all of these experiences can teach you something about what it is like to care for a small child, they won't teach you what it is like to have your very own child. Why not? Because they won't teach you what it is like to have the transformative experience of gestating, producing, and becoming attached to a child of your own. At least in the normal case, if you are a woman who has a child, you go through a distinctive and unique experience when growing, carrying, and giving birth to the child, and in the process you form a particular, distinctive, and unique attachment to the actual newborn you produce.[32] Men go through a partly similar experience, one without the physical part of gestating and giving birth. For both parents, in the normal case, the attachment is then deepened and developed as you raise your child.

Why is the experience unique? Partly because physically producing a child of one's own is unlike any other human experience. As a mother, in a normal pregnancy, you grow the child inside yourself, and produce the baby as part of the birth process. As a father, you

---

[31] Testimony from other parents who've been through the experience is what people are most interested to seek out, but this may in fact be the worst source of information. Gilbert (2007) has a very informative discussion of the way that we make all kinds of mistakes when we try to recall the details of our past experiences.

[32] Wallace (2013).

contribute your genetic material and watch the child grow inside your partner. When a newborn is produced, both parents experience dramatic hormonal changes and enter other new physiological states, all of which help to create the physical realizers for the intensely emotional phenomenology associated with the birth. These experiences contribute to the forming and strengthening of the attachment relation. Further characteristics of the nature of the attachment manifested between you and your child, ones which can have a dramatic effect on the experience of being a parent, are determined by the particular properties of the actual child you produce. All of this generates the unique experience of having one's first child. Before you have had a child of your own, there are at least two new kinds of experience for you to discover: the kind of experience involved in having a child, and the kind of experience involved in having a child of the particular sort that you actually end up having.[33]

Finding these experiences phenomenologically dramatic, especially the experience of giving birth to and meeting your new baby, is normal, and while it may be especially intense for mothers, it can also be very intense for involved fathers. Even "reluctant fathers seek and find redemption in the magic moment of childbirth...Children, once born, can exert a strong pull on the father's emotions" (Edin 2007, pp. 60–1).[34]

Having a child, understood as gestating, producing, and becoming attached to that child, is a unique kind of experience, and this means that the experience of having one's first child is epistemically

---

[33] And it might apply for subsequent children as well, if the subsequent experiences are different enough from the previous experiences.

[34] Even the parent who reacts with numb disbelief or shock upon the presentation of her child has an experience with a uniquely new phenomenal character, despite the fact that the experience does not have the phenomenal character it is "supposed" to have. Indeed, this shocked reaction could have its distinctive character in part *because* it does not have the joyous character the agent was expecting.

transformative.[35] The attachment relation that exists between you and your child, along with its associated properties and the process that led to its creation, is the ground for the special, intense, and distinctive feeling of parental love that new parents experience and for the subjective value of the extended experience of raising that child to adulthood.

There may be a purely biological reason for the distinctive character of the new experience: gestation, birth, and other biological changes contribute to creating physically new states in the parents, especially the mother carrying the child, which in turn cause and realize these new experiences. And even after the birth, when recovering, and when breastfeeding and caring for a child, mothers continue to experience enormous hormonal and other biological changes, while new fathers continue to undergo important physical changes as well. Fans of evolutionary psychology may hold that there is a biological mandate for the physiological changes and physical states that generate the intensely felt attachment to one's offspring.

As I noted above, another cause of the uniqueness of the new experience is the child itself, once he or she exists. The distinctive traits of any particular child, including your own, plus the epistemic fact that you know that this is *your* child, can influence the nature and intensity of your felt attachment.[36] If you cannot know what it will be like to be a parent before you've had a child, this makes the familiar fact that you cannot know the particular properties *your child* will have even more

[35] Although we are really good at making a lot of physical inferences (see, e.g., Battaglia, Hamrick, and Tenenbaum 2013), we are pretty terrible at knowing what it will be like to experience our future emotional states, even when we might be expected to have some sort of idea (Haidt 2006; Gilbert 2007). My point here is that we are in even worse shape when the projection involves a radically new experience.

[36] The physical and emotional generation of the felt attachment to your child grounds the initial subjective value of having a child, and experiencing this attachment, once formed, can be part of the ground for the temporally extended subjective value of having your child.

salient.[37] Not only is it the case that you cannot know what it will be like to be a parent, you cannot know what it will be like to be the parent of the particular child that you will produce.[38] So if you choose to become a parent, when you choose, not only do you not know, in a general sense, what it will be like to be a parent, you don't know what it will be like to have the particular child that you'll end up having. Yet, the particular properties of your future child, her dispositions and inclinations, her health and physical abilities, and her cognitive and emotional makeup will have a *huge* effect on your life as a parent.[39] The character of many hours of your waking life will be composed of experiences that are the direct effects of the features of the actual child that you produce.

In any case, whether the primary basis for your new phenomenology is simply the experience of producing a child, or the particularized experience of producing this particular child, or your first experience of parental love,[40] or being in new physical states that realize new conscious states—or whether it is some complex mix that includes all of these—when you become a parent, you have an experience you've never had before, an experience with an epistemically

[37] Of course, you can know some properties, such as certain genetic properties, given current testing techniques.

[38] For if you could project forward into different possible subjective futures, estimating the different values of what it would be like to have a child with such and such characteristics on the one hand, and so-and-so characteristics on the other, you could at least know something relevant about what the future might be like, and perhaps accommodate your uncertainty about some of the possible outcomes using a range of probability assignments. See the section on imprecise credences in the Afterword for related discussion.

[39] Andrew Solomon (2013) discusses the joys and challenges involved in parenting exceptional children.

[40] I suspect that the creation of this attachment to your child can cause one's first experience of a distinctive natural kind, parental love. Parental love is a kind of love that is distinct from romantic love, filial love, or brotherly love, and is based on the attachment between parent and child, directed from the parent to the child, and, when experienced for the first time, gives rise to a distinctive cognitive

unique character, and in the normal case, one that generates a sustained, intense, felt attachment to the child.[41]

Now, having a child is not just a radically new experience. For many people, it is also a life-changing experience. It might be wonderful, or joyous, or happy—or it might not. But however it is, it is usually very intense, and people who have a child and respond in the normal way find themselves with very different perspectives and preferences after the child is born. That is, for most people, having a child is an epistemically transformative experience that is also personally transformative. Your preferences will change. The way you live your life will change. What and who you care about will change.[42]

And the trouble is, because it is also epistemically transformative to have a child, you don't know how many of your core preferences will evolve. Once you have a child, will you care less about your career or your education? Will your professional work still define your identity? Will you value your child's welfare over your own? Will you love your cat just as much? Will you love your partner more? Will you love your partner less?

Who knows? It depends on what it's like for you to have your child.[43] So when you face the choice of whether you should become

phenomenology. In other words, experiencing parental love for the first time is epistemically analogous to seeing for the first time, or hearing for the first time.

[41] The newness and intensity of the experience was recognized by the New Jersey Supreme Court in the famous 1988 case of Baby M, where a (traditional, not gestational) surrogate mother changed her mind about surrendering her baby. In his opinion, Chief Justice Robert Wilentz (1988) wrote: "Under the contract, the natural mother is irrevocably committed before she knows the strength of her bond with her child. She never makes a totally voluntary, informed decision, for quite clearly any decision prior to the baby's birth is, in the most important sense, uninformed."

[42] "Thirty-year-old TJ...says that motherhood has completely reoriented her life...'I don't see myself as being an individual anymore, really. Everything I do is mostly centered around my children, to make *their* lives better'" (Edin and Kefalas 2007, p. 173). Also see Harman (2009).

[43] "I thought I'd be the perfect mother...It doesn't work that way...Oh, the *reality*," a mother quoted by Edin and Kafalas (2007, p. 159).

a parent, you cannot know what it will be like when you become a parent, nor can you know what it will be like to experience and value the things that you will care about as a parent, or ultimately, know what your preferences, at least in any detailed way, will be. Most of your current preferences about your own future may even fade away, trumped by newly formed preferences about your child's future.

I conclude that having your first child, in many ways, is like becoming a vampire.[44]

We can see this when we realize that, first, you want to make the decision based on the weighted subjective values of the possible outcomes, that is, based on the expected value of the act. And second, since having a child is an experience that is epistemically transformative, you cannot determine the subjective value of what it will be like to have your child before you actually have her. And finally, if the attachment you form to your child is sufficiently strong, the experience is personally transformative, so your core preferences will change, yet you cannot cognitively model how they will change, because you cannot know what it will be like for you to have your child.

As a result, if you have a child, and if your experience is both epistemically and personally transformative, many of your epistemic states will change in subjectively unprojectable ways, and many of these changes will be personally intense, overwhelming, and life-changing.

And this means that you, and anyone who deliberates about having a child in the way we've described, face a profound dilemma. By having a child, you will become first-personally acquainted with a dramatically new experiential kind, and have an experience that will very likely change you into a person who cares about things that are quite different from what you care about now. But until you have the child, you cannot know, from your first personal perspective, what this experience will be like or

---

[44] It's certainly true that in both cases you're in for a lot of sleepless nights.

82

many essential details of how it will change you, since its subjective value will only be revealed once you have irreversibly created your child.

In the absence of experience about what it is like to have a child, then, when you confront the choice of whether to have a child from your first personal perspective, you confront it from a position of deep epistemic ignorance. You cannot, in the relevant way, describe or represent the contours of the state space of the decision problem, nor the outcomes that make up the state space. You cannot describe these features of the state space in the way you'd need to in order to assign them subjective values in an informed way, you cannot determine the states needed for these outcomes, you cannot use your previous experience to predict how your preferences will evolve, nor can you eliminate any probability (or credence) functions from your representor. And so you cannot make your decision in the way we've been describing it, at least, not if you want to meet the normative standard for rationality. This means that, if you want to make the choice rationally, you cannot use the ordinary, culturally sanctioned, subjectively based approach to have a child, the approach where you deliberate about whether to have a child by envisioning what the outcomes involving your lived experience as a parent would be like.

The lesson here is not that the decision to have a child can never be made rationally. The lesson is that, if you've never had a child, *it is impossible to make an informed, rational decision by imagining outcomes based on what it would be like to have your child, assigning subjective values to these outcomes, and then modeling your preferences on this basis.* We cannot proceed by cognitively modeling outcomes concerning these lived experiences, assigning them subjective values, determining our current and future preferences and choosing to maximize expected subjective value, because the transformative nature of the experience blocks this approach. So, the ordinary, natural way to approach this question cannot, for principled reasons, meet the normative rational standard, for, in effect, you are proceeding without sufficient evidence for your evaluation of the desired outcomes. As a result, you cannot rationally

make one of the biggest decisions of your life in the natural, deliberative way you thought you were supposed to make it.

So you cannot rationally decide whether to have your child based
what you think it would be like to have a child, and on how this will
affect your preferences concerning you and your partner and the
other parts of your life, in a suitably informed way. Nor can you use
it to rationally choose to remain childfree. Yet, you must choose anyway—for to avoid making the choice is to choose.

How could common sense have gotten things so wrong? I suspect
that the popular conception of choosing to have a child stems from a
contemporary ideal of personal psychological development through
choice. That is, a modern conception of self-realization involves the
notion that one achieves a kind of maximal self-fulfillment through
making reflective, rational choices about the sort of life one wants to
live, and the choice to have a child (or not) is seen as a paradigmatic
example of such a choice. The rhetoric of the debate over abortion and
medical advances in contraceptive technology have probably also contributed to the framing of the decision to have a child as a personal,
deliberate choice. While such notions of personal fulfillment and
self-realization through reflective choice might be apt for whether one
chooses to grow one's own vegetables, what music one listens to, or
whether one does yoga, it is not apt for the choice to have a child.

The situation is perfectly parallel to the other cases of deliberative choice in transformative contexts that we've been considering. If
you are not and never have been deaf, you can't follow the normative
standard for rational decision-making if you choose to give your child
a cochlear implant based on the belief that what it is like to hear is
better than what it is like to be deaf. And if you are a deaf person who
does not have and has never had species-typical hearing, you can't follow the normative standard for rational decision-making if you reject
a cochlear implant for your child based on the belief that what it is like
for her to be deaf is better than what it would be like for her to be able
to hear. One cannot make informed, rational decisions in these cases
without access to the right kind of evidence.

Are there other ways to make transformative decisions that can meet the normative standard? Yes. One way to make such a decision is to dispense with subjective deliberation and so to dispense with a decision involving subjective values altogether.

Let's look at this strategy using the case of choosing to have a child. In the past, non-subjective facts and circumstances played a much larger role in the causal process leading up to parenthood. Before contraceptive devices were widely available, deliberation didn't play the same role. Often, you just ended up having a child. And to the extent you actively chose to have children, often it was because you needed an heir, or needed more hands to work the farm, or whatever. But this is not the contemporary approach. If, as a member of an affluent, contemporary Western culture, you dispense with subjective deliberation and subjective values in today's world, you reject a central tenet of that culture's ordinary way of thinking about the choice.[45]

Perhaps we should find a modern equivalent to the old-school way. For example, instead of deciding to have a child simply because that's what one is supposed to do, or instead of making a decision based on what you think it would be like to have a child, perhaps you should make the decision based on scientific evidence. The suggestion isn't that you merely weigh the empirical evidence in conjunction with your personal deliberations about what it's like to have a child, because we have already seen that you don't know what it'd be like for you to have a child. The idea is that, instead of trying to assess subjective values and use them in your deliberation, you make the decision based *solely* on the available empirical research, for example, research that compares life satisfaction and well-being for those who have children to those who do not.

Now, the available empirical information isn't fine-grained enough to tell you exactly how someone with your particular psychological characteristics would respond to the change, but the results seem to apply to a wide variety of individuals. Across the board, while the

---

[45] See Zelizer (1985) for the classic account of how children have come to be regarded as emotionally priceless.

highs seem to be higher for parents, the lows seem to be lower, and many measures suggest that parents with children in the home, especially mothers of young children, have lower levels of overall subjective well-being. Moreover, individuals who have never had children report similar levels of life satisfaction as individuals with grown children who have left home.[46]

The empirical work suggests two conclusions. First, it provides evidence for the claim that having a child is epistemically and personally transformative. Prospective parents often choose to have a child because they suppose it will uncontroversially increase their levels of happiness and subjective well-being. The evidence undermines that supposition.[47]

Second, if you are prepared to ignore all of your subjective assessments about what it would be like for you to have a child, and choose

[46] The negative impact of children on happiness and life satisfaction has been widely discussed in sociology, psychology, and economics. McClanahan and Adams (1989) describe how a number of studies "suggest that parenthood has negative consequences for the psychological well-being of adults." One analysis of survey data covering a wide range of the empirical sociological results concerning parenthood indicates there isn't any group of parents, including those whose children have grown and left home, where those groups are determined by standard sociological classifications such as income, marital status, gender, race, education, and mental health, with higher levels of overall emotional well-being than non-parents (Evenson and Simon 2005; Simon 2008). Psychological results are more mixed, but most studies report that parents have lower levels of subjective well-being (Kahneman et al. 2004). The research does show that marital status, education, and financial status influence the degree to which parenthood impacts emotional well-being. For more, see Nomaguchi and Milkie (2003); Kahneman et al. (2004); Kahneman and Kreuger (2006); and Nelson et al. (2013); and see Simon (2008) for an overall summary.

[47] "The transition to parenthood represents a transformation not simply of the parents as individuals but of the developing family system...(the main domains for possible changes): are (a) the quality of relationships in the new parents' families of origin, (b) the quality of the new parents' relationship as a couple, (c) the quality of relationship that each parent develops with the baby, (d) the balance between life stress and social support in the new family, and (e) the well-being or distress of each parent and child as individuals. Taken as a group, studies of the transition to

solely on the basis of the empirical research, if you want to maximize your expected subjective value, the research (to the extent that there are clear results) suggests you should not have a child. If we simply follow the dominant empirical conclusions of the experts, it seems that *anyone* who wants to make a rational decision about parenthood that is based on maximizing expected subjective value must either suspend judgment (given the lack of a clear consensus on the results), or should actively choose to remain childless.

This, of course, is a disastrous solution.

It is disastrous partly because it suggests that you cannot rationally choose to have a child. It is also disastrous because it implies that the best way to rationally make this decision is to eliminate any consideration of your own cognitive phenomenology when deciding whether to have a child. Prescribing this way of making the choice as a solution to the problem implies that, when making one of the biggest decisions in your life, your own personal beliefs and preferences about your future lived experience must be ignored.

Unless robots have taken over the world when humans weren't looking, for many of us, this is an untenable way to approach choices involving our personal goals, hopes, projects, and dreams. In other words, in today's society, when making important personal choices, we want to consult our own, personal preferences and to reflect on what we want our future lives to be like as part of assigning values to outcomes. It is simply unacceptable to be expected to give up this sort of personal autonomy in order to make decisions about how one wants to live one's life.

Imagine Sally, who has always believed that having a child would bring her happiness and fulfillment, deciding not to have a child simply because the empirical evidence tells her she will maximize her expected subjective value by choosing to remain childless. For her

parenthood show that new parents experience shifts in all five domains." Common responses to having a child include negative changes in relationships and increases in distress and stress levels. Cowan and Cowan (1995, pp. 413–14).

to choose this way, ignoring her subjective preferences and relying solely on external reasons, seems bizarre. How could Sally's own preferences not matter to her decision? If Sally, in effect, turns her decision over to the experts and eliminates consideration of her first personal perspective, she seems to be giving up her autonomy for the sake of rationality.

Even Lisa, who, let us suppose, never wanted to have a child, but decides not to have a child based solely on the empirical evidence, is not choosing in an acceptable way. Her choice, if rational, has nothing to do with her personal preferences to not have a child. Lisa does not have special insight into how she'd be as a parent: instead, she merely gets lucky. It just so happens that her preferences support the same alternative as the evidence does. Both of these examples bring out how rejecting the subjective perspective in favor of impersonal, "big data" reasoning is not an appealing or plausible option.

Perhaps you think that you can circumvent the problem of epistemic and personal transformation and the problem of retaining autonomy by using the empirical data in conjunction with making your own "informed" choice. You may think you have special insight into your situation, so you can build in your own beliefs and preferences after all. That is, you might think that the right way to draw on empirical research is not to use it as a *replacement* for your own deliberation, but as a *supplement* to inform and guide your assessment of whether you want to have a child. Perhaps you also have testimony from your friends and relatives, all of whom assure you that they are very glad that they chose to become parents, and that they cannot imagine life without their children. Perhaps they also tell you that they are sure that you, too, will feel this way once you become a parent, and you think that you should use their testimony as evidence to guide your deliberations.

But employing this strategy, as I noted at the outset, will get you right back into trouble. We've already seen that you are not rationally justified in assigning subjective values to outcomes concerning what it would be like for you to have a child. Assigning values based on your personal judgments in tandem with considerations drawn from the empirical research doesn't make the values based on your personal judgments any more rational. The only evidential basis for your assignments is that which you are justified in having, and that does not include phenomenal evidence for your subjective values and evolving preferences based on what it is like to have a child. To make the decision rational, the empirical guide must *replace* your subjective deliberations, not merely "inform" them.

Testimony from your friends and relatives suffers from related defects. First, such testimony is notoriously unreliable—people are terrible at assessing decisions they've made (scientists use sophisticated survey techniques to try to circumvent this problem).[48] And claims like "I can't imagine life without my child" are not evidence that having a child has high subjective value; they are merely evidence that having a child impairs a parent's psychological ability to envision certain counterfactual scenarios. (See Harman (2009) for a related point.)

Second, unless you know which characteristics you need to have in order to have an outcome with a high subjective value, you won't know how to evaluate the anecdotal testimony from your friends and family. You don't know which psychological similarities and differences between you and your friends and family are the ones that would be relevant to increases in well-being or happiness, and there isn't any well-documented empirical work showing correlations between personalities of a particular type and increases in well-being or happiness after having a child. (You might think that liking other peoples' children or being a homebody might be correlated to increased happiness and well-being, but there is no evidence to support this sort of speculative folk intuition. Given this, using such speculations to support the choice to have a child is little more rational than consulting a star chart for astrological guidance.)

---

[48] Gilbert (2007); and Kahneman (2013).

There is another wrinkle with relying on testimony from friends and relatives. Having a child is an intense experience that changes your perspective, forming new core preferences and beliefs. Often, people will testify that, as a direct result of having their children, their preferences related to being a parent change. So, while your friends and relatives might be able to honestly, truthfully, and enthusiastically report to you that *now* their preferences are better satisfied than they'd have been if they hadn't had children, their preferences may have arisen *simply because they had children in the first place*.

In other words, if such testimony provides any evidence at all, it is evidence that having a child can change you in a way so that the preferences you will form as the result of having your child will be satisfied. But this is not evidence that you should consult if you want to satisfy your current preferences. This is evidence that, if you have a child, you will form new preferences that will then be satisfied by having the child. (Often, you form a preference to have the child you actually have.) If the preferences being satisfied are the newly formed preferences that resulted from having children, such testimony from friends and relatives does not provide evidence that you, with the preferences you have right now, should have a child.

In fact, what much of the evidence suggests is that people who have never had children have preferences such that, if they knew what it was like to have a child *and retained their pre-child preferences*, they would not choose to have a child. Yet, the process of having a child changes people, such that, having had a child, almost nobody wants to go back to their pre-child self. Parents are more like vampires than we might think: no one would want to become a vampire while retaining their human feelings and preferences (partly for reasons that are indescribable to humans), and no vampire would want to become human again.[49]

Perhaps you think the right response to the possibility of preference change is to choose to have a child. After all, in virtue of having the child,

<hr/>

[49] I'm indebted to discussion with John Quiggin here.

you will form preferences that, whatever they will be, will be such that they are satisfied by what it's like for you to have a child. So you think it's best to ignore your current first-order preferences, whatever they are.

This leads back to the problem we discussed in chapter 2, the problem of how to rationally decide between the preferences of the pre-change self and the (potentially) post-changed self. Standard decision theory holds that the rational decision-maker must choose in order to maximize her expected value given her *current* preferences.[50] Adopting some sort of higher-order preference to prefer the preferences of the later self might give you the result you want in this case, but it is not a rule that can be followed in a principled way.[51] One problem is that you don't know what your new preferences will be, so it is unclear what the justification for preferring them is. Another problem is that ignoring your current preferences and choosing to have a child because you know that, however your preferences change, they will be satisfied, seems no more defensible than, say, taking a drug that makes you less intelligent, yet has the happy effect that once you are less intelligent you will prefer being in that (ignorant but blissful) state, or willfully becoming an addict merely because, once you are addicted, you will prefer to satisfy your drug-induced cravings.

There is a different way to respond to the empirical results. In chapter 2, we discussed a kind of subjective value we assign to experiences because we value the discovery of what it is like to have them. The valuation need not be based on how pleasurable the experience is, nor

[50] Moss (2015) argues persuasively that what is rationally permissible or obligatory for the decision-maker at a time is entirely determined by her mental states at that time. Also see Hedden (2015).

[51] As Richard Pettigrew pointed out to me, if you are prepared to dispense with your current preferences in order to take on new preferences, in what sense are your current preferences really your preferences? Compare Jon Elster (1997, p. 754), who remarks, "I believe, however, that the very idea of intentional change of time preference is incoherent...to want to be motivated by long-term concerns is ipso facto to be motivated by long term concerns."

need it be just a value based on the qualitative feel of the experience. The value is, instead, based on the revelation the experience involves. Perhaps part of the value of some experiences comes from what they teach us.

The suggestion is that some experiences, especially those that seem to connect in important ways to deep facts about the human condition, or those that seem to teach us information about the nature of moral or aesthetic facts, have subjective value in virtue of what they teach us through the discovery of lived experience, a value that extends past their first-order qualitative character. In chapter 2, I described these sorts of experiences as *revelatory*, and suggested that we value them for the information we gain about the intrinsic nature of the experience when we experience it. Compare Aristotle, in the Metaphysics: "All men by nature desire to know. An indication of this is the delight we take in our senses; for even apart from their usefulness they are loved for themselves..."[52]

We can discover the intrinsic nature of a sensory experience such as what it is like to see red merely by seeing red for the first time. But cognitively richer revelations are also possible, for example, the revelation of discovering what it is like to live a certain kind of life. This sort of richer revelation can be created by a wide range of experiences, such as experiences involving suffering or horror, experiences of aesthetic beauty, and experiences of acting selflessly or generously. It can also be involved in having extended experiences such as those involving great accomplishment or sustained effort. If there is subjective value in having certain kinds of experiences, a subjective value that comes apart from whether such experiences contribute to one's first-order happiness and well-being or whether they involve pleasure or pain, then one might choose to have that kind of experience for the sake of having it. That is, we might choose to have an experience

---

[52] Here I am also drawing on Lewis (1988); Johnston (1992); and Johnston (1992); and Campbell (1993), but using the notion of revelation for my own ends. Lewis (1988) argues that experience can give us information, and Johnston (1992) and Campbell (1993) describe how seeing a color seems to be revelatory, in that it seems to teach us something. (Whether the color experience actually teaches us about the color we experience is not my concern here.)

because of its revelatory character, rather than choosing it because what it is like to have it is in some way pleasurable or enjoyable.

I think there is something that is right about this—we do sometimes choose to have experiences purely because of their revelatory character, and we may also choose to avoid experiences for the same reason. I will come back to this in the next chapter.

In the context of evaluating social scientific conclusions about parenthood and well-being, what the possibility of revelation suggests is that empirical work that seems to show that parents experience lower levels of happiness and subjective well-being may not be giving us a complete picture. The experience of becoming a parent and raising a child may have intrinsic subjective value, that is, revelatory value, even if it makes parents less happy and reduces their well-being on many of the usual measures. The idea is that something about living the experience, that is, having the extended experience of being a parent in terms of living through this experience, is revelatory.

Thinking about the decision this way seems to capture part of what, intuitively, many parents want to say about the value of having a child, and, at least arguably, can allow prospective parents to shrug off the disturbing results from the scientific literature. In addition to providing a satisfying response to the empirical literature, it cements the role of cognitive phenomenology in personal decision-making, making it clear that the decision must include considerations drawn from one's personal perspective and subjective values.

Unfortunately, however, focusing on the subjective value of having a revelatory experience won't solve our decision-theoretic problems with the transformative choice to have a child, because we've simply characterized the unknown subjective value of what it's like to have a child as an unknown subjective value of the revelatory character of living the experience (a value, recall, that need not be a hedonic value based on happiness, pleasure, or pain).

You still have to make the decision without having the relevant information about the expected subjective value. You still don't know how revelatory the life experience will be, or what the character of the revelation will be like, and, as a result, you don't know the range of possible subjective values. You also still don't know what it will be like to live the life of the person you will become if you have a child, so you are still facing the possibility of forming unknown new preferences, and so the higher-order worry about which preferences to respect (your current ones, or the new ones you'd have as a parent) remains.

## Temporally Extended Selves

I have been discussing experiences involving immediate, sharp transitions, but transformative experiences can involve change that occurs over a period of time, or occurs in the distant future from the time at which you must make the decision to act. In this way, ordinary approaches towards central, life-defining choices, like the choice to get married, the choice to adopt and parent a young child into adulthood, and the choice of a career, can involve transformative choices. Here, you must make a choice that affects your temporally extended self, a choice to initiate an experience that lasts for months or years, or your current time slice must make a choice that determines the lived experience of a time slice in your distant future.

Imagine that, after years of searching and many disappointing dates, you finally meet your soul mate. You meet the person who seems, to you, to embody everything you were looking for in a partner. As you get to know this person, you fall deeply in love, you can't imagine life without them, and you see all the personality traits and dispositions that you think a potential spouse should have. The two of you start to discuss marriage, and you think carefully and reflectively about whether to take the plunge—should you get married?

When you think about whether to marry someone, you are supposed to reflect on whether you truly love this person—whether they are "The One." Do you love them, truly, deeply, madly? Are they the

right person for you, the one you want to spend your life with, building a life together, perhaps even buying a house, having children, and
doing other things that married couples do? Perhaps less importantly,
do your friends approve? And perhaps even less importantly—but
still relevantly—do your parents and other family members approve?

Your deliberation about whether to get married, then, involves reflection on whether you should decide to establish a long-term, potentially
permanent relationship with another person. When you marry someone, you are not just deciding to be married at that time, or for just that
week. (Setting aside celebrities, of course.) You are deciding whether
you want to commit yourself to an extended life event. As such, it is a
decision to establish a relationship between an extended future temporal segment of yourself with an extended future temporal segment of
another person. You aren't just marrying them for the here and now,
you are marrying this person for the long term, deciding to be with
them over an extended time period, to be part of their life as they grow
and change, "for better, for worse, for richer, for poorer, in sickness and
in health, until death do us part." In other words, you are deciding to
share your future with this person. When two people decide to get
married, then, each makes a decision about their extended future self,
deciding to pair it with another person's extended future self.

So when you reflect on whether to get married, it is a reflection on
whether to to pair your extended future self with another extended
future self, and includes deliberation on whether this pairing, intended
to last through life's ups and downs, will provide happiness and life
satisfaction for both of you.

Is such a decision rational? It may not be, if it is made based on this
sort of deliberation. You are making your decision by attempting to
project forward into your subjective future, to see what it will be like
for you to make a life with this person. If you have lived with your
prospective spouse for many years, perhaps you know enough about
what they are like, and so enough about what your future lived experience would be like, to know what it would be like to have an extended
marriage with them.

But in the case we are considering, it's not clear you know enough. You might know enough about your soul mate to know that they would make you happy in the short term, and know in a general way about what it will be like in the near future to be married to this person. But what you don't know is what your long-term, temporally extended married life will be like, especially if you have never been married before. This is because, first, forming and developing this relationship changes who you are, especially over time, by transforming your values and personal preferences. The attachment you form to your spouse changes how you view yourself, how you respond to others in your life, and what you care about for the future.[53] Second, the various challenges, the ups and downs you will experience in your relationship, are usually not foreseeable and involve new kinds of experiences from those you had when you were single, yet they can have a huge effect on what your marriage is like.

The point is that, in virtue of forming this sort of attachment to another person, your response to events may change you so much that you cannot predict what the marriage, in the long term, will be like. If, in ten years, your spouse is diagnosed with cancer, how will you respond? How will it affect your marriage? What if your spouse loses their job, or if you are permanently disabled by a car accident? What if your spouse becomes rich and successful, while your career stagnates? This is part of the point of the marriage ceremony, to bring out how, when you marry, you are not marrying someone based on knowing what your future life will be like. You are marrying them based on the commitment to discover a future life together. When you marry, you take on commitments that involve providing support even through unexpected changes and the many new kinds of events that life brings, and you face these new experiences as an attached person, not as a single person. If you choose to marry, many new kinds of experiences will cause you to develop and build your relationship with your spouse in whatever way you and that other person, with their particular psychological profile and preferences, react to these events.

[53] Kolodny (2003); Wallace (2013).

You probably have some idea of how the person you are about to marry will initially respond to stressful or important life issues, and of your own capacity for managing these different situations. But, especially if new kinds of major life events change your preferences, you can't know what it will be like to actually experience these events with this person, as they will be in the future, or what it will be like to experience the extended relationship that will actually result from facing new kinds of experiences as a married couple. So while you can know some things before you get married, such as your prospective spouse's current dispositions and inclinations, you cannot know what it will be like to have the marriage that you will actually have. In such a case, a marriage is an extended transformative experience.

In this important sense, choosing to get married can require you to choose without knowing what the future you are choosing will be like. The decision involves making a commitment, after forming the attachment to your spouse, to discovery: that is, however you discover the experience to be, you will be a full participant in the temporally extended event of your marriage, such that you, together with your spouse, face whatever revelation your married life will bring. (Sometimes the preference change that discovery brings results in divorce.)

The kind of discovery involved in making an extended-life commitment comes out even more clearly when you decide to become a parent, that is, when you commit to parenting a child from a young age to adulthood and beyond. Perhaps you are deciding whether you want to get pregnant or whether to adopt. Above, I argued that having a child by physically producing a baby and raising her to adulthood is an experience that is epistemically and personally transformative. But the extended experience of raising a child, the kind of experience that is had by biological and by adoptive parents, and one where a person becomes a parent in the fullest sense of the word, is itself epistemically and personally transformative.

When you become a parent, you decide to engage with, support and guide another person's life. Often, in the process of being a parent, you develop a long-term, loving relationship with your child, one that is more nuanced than the sort of initial, intense love you'd feel for a new-born. The extended temporal process of being a parent involves becoming the sort of person who experiences a new kind of non-romantic, caring love for a child, along with a corresponding vulnerability.

What you choose when you choose to become a parent is to become attached to a child in a special new way, and this changes both the way that you respond to the events that arise in your life and the sorts of events that you may have to face. One of the greatest fears of a parent is that their child will be killed or seriously injured, and as a parent, one must learn to live with the fear and the emotional vulnerability this entails. The unselfish love you feel for your child, the willing desire to sacrifice your time, money, career, and even—if it came to it—your life itself, is an experience that many can only feel by raising a child. Such changes in how you feel and how you live, when you become a parent, have major effects on your lived experience and your short- and long-term preferences.

Another concrete way you might think you should approach and plan your future is by deliberately choosing a career. The choice to embark on a particular career path is a choice to have a particular sort of life or become a particular sort of person. If the career is a professional one or requires significant training, your choice to become a member of that profession may not be realized for many years.

Consider the choice to become a doctor. Could you simply drift into a medical career, idly taking classes in organic chemistry, memorizing anatomical details for fun, then suddenly realizing that you are prepared to take the MCAT (Medical College Admission Test)? After doing unexpectedly well on the test, you end up going to medical school just see what it is like, and then just happen to pass all your exams?

Of course not. This isn't the way it works at all. Becoming a doctor requires a high level of commitment, focus and planning, not to mention luck and hard work. Simply to be eligible for admission you have to take a rigorous series of college-level science and mathematics courses in order to demonstrate your capacity for problem-solving and for grasping scientific and medical concepts, and to prepare for medical exams and courses. You also need to achieve high grades, to participate in extracurricular activities, to perform well on the admissions exams, and to somehow demonstrate evidence of character, integrity, and well-roundedness. If all goes well, and you make good choices, and if you are lucky and you work hard, you might get accepted to medical school.

Gaining admission to medical school is just the start. You'll then have years of medical training, including several years of being an intern and resident, depending on your specialty. Medical school and residency are grueling experiences that require you to set aside other pursuits and focus almost entirely on your training and performance. The work is all-encompassing, and requires significant personal and financial sacrifice. And it will change you. The process of becoming a doctor involves significant personal changes, some of which are part of an intended socialization of the individual.[54]

When you consider an important career choice like this, you are supposed to reflect carefully on what kind of person you are and what kind of person you want to become. You are expected to evaluate your hopes, dreams, and aspirations. You are to think of what you want to spend your life doing, about what sort of career would make you happy and give you long-lasting life satisfaction. One doesn't make the decision to train as a physician, or to train for any other highly specialized, competitive occupation, lightly.

You may also seek out advice. Perhaps your mother has strong feelings on the matter. Your guidance counselor will tell you whether you have the traits you need to succeed in your attempt, and may suggest that you reflect on whether you have the inner drive and other personal characteristics needed for such a demanding career. If you are thinking of becoming a doctor, he might ask whether you can handle the sight of blood, and how you manage stress and decision-making under pressure.

[54] The classic description of the socialization of medical students in the mid twentieth century presents a useful perspective on this issue: Becker, Geer, Hughes, and Strauss (1961).

You might also consider the larger picture. Most societies hold doctors in high esteem, rewarding them with respect, social prestige, and financial remuneration. People who become doctors often seem to be happy, successful members of society. They are financially comfortable. They are contributing to the overall social good by helping others. They perform an essential social service by providing medical care to the population. It's a career that carries a lot of positives with it, and at least from a cultural perspective, doctors seem to be very satisfied with their personal choices.[55] It isn't the sort of career that people drop out of once they have obtained their degrees and finished their training. The rewards are great, and your mother will be proud of you, bragging about your success to all her friends.

But of course, while these facts may influence your choice, you shouldn't become a doctor merely because it would make your parents happy and because you'd make a lot of money. And you shouldn't become a doctor merely because it is a way to help other people. All of these considerations may carry weight, of course. But what also matters, in this case, is what *you* want.

When you choose a career, you are supposed to choose something that fits who you are—something that fits your personality and disposition, and that you would enjoy doing. Your career needs to suit the type of person you are, and most importantly, it should be something that you will find rewarding over the course of your life. You want your career to provide life satisfaction and the happiness that comes with it, in addition to providing something you can live on and having social value.

This is why we accord respect to the person who decides that, after reflection, being a doctor is not for her. Not everyone should become a doctor. Perhaps you recoil at the thought of seeing blood, or you don't like to touch other people. Perhaps you would rather be a teacher.

[55] Although as Neil Levy pointed out to me, doctors also have a very high suicide rate.

Perhaps you would rather live in a city and study drama or painting. Perhaps your dream is to be a physicist, or a biologist, or a concert violinist.

If you ignore your own inclinations and choose to become a doctor because society values doctors, because it's a job that involves helping people, because your parents wanted you to become a doctor, and because you notice that doctors testify that they are happy with their choice (perhaps your guidance counselor gives you a handbook that reports "99% of doctors are satisfied with their career choice"), intuitively, it feels like you are making a mistake.

This is because it seems strange to decide to become a doctor without consulting your own views about whether you would like to be one. Making such an important choice without consulting your personal preferences is, at best, unusual. Many people would think you were misguided, making the decision for the wrong reasons: choosing to be a doctor because other people thought you should, or because it is the right choice for most people. The right choice for most people might not be the right choice for you, and in order to determine whether it is the right choice, you have to consult your own inclinations, your own desires and your own preferences for your future.

Even worse, if you secretly had no desire at all to become a doctor, or even thought that you would hate being a doctor, but still decided to become a doctor, your choice is, normatively speaking, obviously wrong. You are not being true to yourself if you choose something merely because you will end up in a group of wealthy, satisfied people who contribute to society. What social group you might end up in is probably a factor in your choice, but it shouldn't be the only thing that matters when you make up your mind.

So, well before you become a doctor, you need to make the decision to pursue a medical career, and to do this, you need to determine whether what it would be like for you to be a doctor is what you want your future life to be like. But the problem is that the experience of becoming a doctor is transformative, and thus what it is like to be a doctor is subjectively or first-personally unknowable until it is experienced. If you make the choice to become a doctor, when you choose, you cannot even know in a generalized first personal way about what it will be like for you, many years in the future, to be a doctor, or what your evolved preferences in these new circumstances will be. Moreover, you cannot know what it will be like for you to participate in more fine grained kinds of future events, such as what it will be like for you to respond to particular life-threatening situations or to be responsible for trying to save the life of another human being. The particular properties of what it will be like, for example, to be in the emergency room, faced with the brutal facts of life and death, or to have to tell parents their three-year-old child is dead—will have a *huge* effect on your life as a doctor. The character of many hours of your waking life will be composed of experiences that are the direct effects of the features of the career that you have chosen. But you can't perform the requisite cognitive modeling, because you don't have the experience you need to know what these different lived experiences would be like.

If career choices and other choices involving extended temporal selves or selves in the distant future can be transformative, they cannot be made rationally by assigning subjective values and determining preferences based on envisioning the character of possible future experiences. A choice on this basis is not even rationally permissible, for you cannot use subjective-value-based reasons to guide your choice between acts if you cannot know the subjective values of the outcomes themselves. If you can't know the values of the outcomes of, say, choosing a career as a violinist and choosing a career as a doctor, you cannot compare them nor even grasp enough information about them to choose in a rationally permissible way.[56] The problem is not, in such a case, that we can assign values to the outcomes but think they are somehow incommensurable: the

---

[56] They are "noncomparable" outcomes in Ruth Chang's (1997) sense: you aren't in a position to successfully compare or substantively fail in your attempt to compare them.

problem is that we cannot assign subjective values at all, nor predict how our preferences will evolve in response to the choice, and thus we cannot determine our preferences about the acts in any meaningful sense.[57]

Choosing to have a child, choosing a cochlear implant, or choosing a new career are very naturally understood as involving choices concerning acts that lead to deep, extensive personal transformations resulting in fundamental changes in personal preferences. But, as I've been emphasizing, such experiences may not just be personally transformative: they may also be epistemically transformative. If so, a choice involving such an experience is a transformative choice. If you have been deaf from birth, you will have dramatically new kinds of experiences and undergo significant personal changes if you receive a cochlear implant. Having your first child is a radically new experience, full of intense love and crushing responsibility, changing much about what you care about. A decision to become a doctor happens long before you know what it is like to take charge in a life-threatening situation, or to respond to a dying person in great pain, and before you know what kind of person you'll become as a result of your intensive training.

These cases, and many others, involve the decision to make a transformative choice. Choices like whether to get a cochlear implant, whether to have a child, or whether to pursue a medical career embed the very same problematic structure as the choice of whether to become a vampire. So we must not set cases of transformative choice to one side in order to concentrate on the things that "really" matter.

I have been arguing that transformative choices involve decisions concerning an epistemically and personally transformative

---

[57] Joseph Raz (1988) discusses a case where one must choose between a career as a lawyer and a career as a clarinetist, but assumes that we can know enough about the outcomes to know their values (and, according to his view, to know the values are incommensurable).

experience. For the sake of clarity and argument, I've focused on a few special cases where the transformative nature of the experience is easily identifiable. There are many other kinds of experience that qualify: one that needs special mention, and deserves more extensive discussion, is the case of religious experience.[58]

Moreover, while there are experiences that are clearly and determinately transformative, there may also be experiences that are transformative only to some degree. If transformative experiences can come in degrees, whether they involve abrupt transitions or gradual ones, then the lessons I've drawn from the types of transformative experience I've discussed may apply to many cases of everyday decision-making.

What the discussion of transformative choice highlights is how, for each of us, facing such choice is a pervasive and important part of living a life. As you navigate your life's course, you must make a series of choices to have (or to avoid) new experiences and to discover preferences that reveal themselves to you only once you've had the experiences that determine them. As a rational and reflective decision-maker, you should recognize the challenges these choices raise, and understand how these experiences may change you into a different kind of person, a person who cares about things that are very different from what you care about now.

[58] See my (n.d.) "Transformative religious belief."

CHAPTER 4

# THE SHOCK OF THE NEW

As an authentic, rational agent, you are expected to take charge of your own destiny. You chart your future, deliberating and reflecting on who you really are and what you really want from life, and, once you've determined your preferences, you determine the right course and act accordingly. You live an authentic life by faithfully modeling your preferences, and you live a rational life by matching your choices to these preferences. Rational authenticity, then, is hewing as close as you can to the kind of life that best realizes your dreams, hopes, and aspirations.[1]

When we think of ourselves as agents, we think of ourselves as located at a point in time and space, with a conscious, centered point of view that looks out from that point to the rest of the world. From this centered, first personal perspective, we consider the appeal of various acts we might perform by reflecting on our past, consulting the information we have in our present, and mapping our possible causal paths forward into the future. At each experienced moment, we generate a continuously updating map of possible futures for ourselves, a map that evolves over time, as we move from the present into the future, in response to input from our perceptions and decisions. As such, an agent's point of view is a locus or centered personal perspective in a subjective present, from which she projectively models different possible futures stemming from different possible choices she could make.[2]

---

[1] This is a cultural notion prevalent in wealthy Western societies.
[2] I share this way of framing things with Jenann Ismael, and here I draw on her (forthcoming) "Passage, flow and the logic of temporal perspectives."

105

From this perspective, then, as a conscious agent, you experience yourself as deciding which future to bring into actuality. "We experience the world as an open system with a fixed past and a future that (in the literal sense) awaits decision."[3] And as an agent occupying your distinctive first personal perspective on the world, you use your evolving perspective to navigate your life's path, from moment to moment, from birth to death. You use your memories from the past, your beliefs about the present, and your anticipations about possible subjective futures to formulate your current and evolving self, as well as to develop temporally extended, forward-looking, subjective projections about what will happen. In this way, you experience yourself as a located, conscious self with control over who you are and how you evolve by making choices, at each experienced present, to perform or avoid particular acts.[4]

When you make your choices, then, you make them from your first personal perspective, recalling what you know from past experience, drawing on information you have about the nature of the world from your own experience (as well as from science and other reliable sources), and making decisions in your present in order to bring about a particular future. Based on what you know, you consider various subjective futures for yourself that your choice might bring about, that is, you consider how, from your present point of view, your life in the immediate future and perhaps through to a distant future is most likely to develop if you choose to perform one act rather than another.

When you consider what might happen in your future, your consideration involves an imaginative reflection on what it will be like, from your point of view, to experience the series of future events that are the mostly likely outcomes of whatever it is that you choose to do.

---

[3] Ismael (forthcoming).

[4] As I have argued in previous chapters, this fits very naturally with cognitive approaches to causal modeling and causal learning.

You use this reflection on what you think these events will be like, that is, what you think your lived experience will be like, to authentically determine your preferences about your future, and thus to decide how to rationally act in the present. This is an intuitive and ordinary way to determine the subjective values for each decision you make—by cognitively modeling the various possible outcomes and what those outcomes mean to you, the decision-maker, as the primary experiencer of the effects of your acts, and it fits our philosophical account of the responsible, rational agent.

So there is a clear philosophical underpinning for the powerful sense of control and authenticity that we get by thinking in specific and particular terms about the different subjective futures that our different possible choices could bring about, and then carefully evaluating and choosing between these different futures by assessing their value, determining which future we prefer, and authoritatively choosing the act that is most likely to bring it about. If we act in accordance with our preferences, by comparing acts with different expected values and choosing to act in a way that maximizes our expected value, then authenticity, agential control, and reflective assessment are guided by the normative rational standard, giving us a normative picture that pairs authentic, deliberative reasoning with rational choice and action.

But, as I have argued, the fact that many of our big life decisions concern experiences that are both epistemically and personally transformative threatens to rip this picture apart. In cases of transformative choice, the rationality of the approach to life where we authoritatively control our choices by attempting to subjectively project ourselves forward and consider possible subjective futures is undermined by our epistemic limitations on knowing what our future experiences and preferences will be like. Our modern desire to own our futures when we face such choices, a desire that is expressed by the way we reflect and deliberate over which life's path we want to take, cannot be satisfied.

Transformative choice raises these problems because our individual decision-making perspective sits at the nexus where our conscious present evolves from memory towards expectation, but making our decisions from this mental position is incompatible with the third-personal perspective that implicitly defines the standard for normative rational action.

Just at the point where we must decide how to navigate from the present into the future using our first personal perspective, we are confronted by the impossibility of assigning subjective values to future outcomes. The problem, at its heart, derives from the way our models for rational agency and decision have been implicitly framed in third personal terms. The way this stymies our subjective perspective, as a first personal perspective embedded in the present and projecting itself forward in time, can be drawn out by a distinction between two ways you can regard the outcome of an act you will perform.

The first way you can regard the outcome is in descriptive, causal terms, described from a third personal, tenseless perspective. For example, if at time t1, you choose to become a vampire, you know that at time t2, you'll become a new kind of creature, one with new sensory perceptions and desires. Or, if you are profoundly deaf at t1 and decide to receive a cochlear implant, you know your actions will cause you to be able hear a wide range of sounds at some future time t2. If you decide to become a parent, you know that in the future you'll have to care for a small child and that you'll experience a new sense of responsibility.

From this third-personal perspective, you know no more about your future self than anybody else does. For example, at the time when you contemplate your choice to get a cochlear implant, one way in which you know your future involves hearing sound is that you'll know you'll satisfy a description "hearing sound." But this third personal descriptive knowledge is no more substantial than the way that another profoundly deaf person who has never heard sound knows that, in the future, you will hear sound. The third-personal way that you know you will have these properties involves knowing them in a way that anybody else, even someone who has never had experiences resembling your experiences, knows that your future self will have them.

Compare this to regarding the outcome in a first personal way. If you know what it's like to hear sound, say, because you were once able to hear, when you contemplate your choice to get a cochlear implant, you know what it's like to satisfy the description "hearing sound," and so you can assign a subjective value to the outcome of becoming a hearer. But if you have never heard sound, you can't assign a subjective value to this outcome, and the difference in experience is the basis for the asymmetry. The first personal way that you know you will have the property of hearing sound involves knowing this in a way that only someone who has had experiences resembling your experiences can know.

What you care about, when making a decision about your own personal future, is not the third personal descriptive knowledge that you will have certain properties in the future, but your experience-based first personal knowledge of what it will be like for you to have these properties. In other words, you care about what it will be like for *you* to experience *your* future, because you want to determine *your* preferences in terms of *your* expected subjective values. For example, maximizing your expected subjective value of becoming a species-typical hearer is what you care about when you make the decision to get a cochlear implant.

When we confront the decision to become a vampire, or to have a child, or to become a violinist, and so on, from our first personal perspective, a third-personal way of assessing and modeling the experiential outcomes is often insubstantial and unhelpful, because it merely involves describing the experiences, not determining their subjective values. The special, first personal sense in which you know what it will be like to experience the likely results of your choice is the sense that fits with our centered perspective on the world and is reflected in our subjective values.

If you cannot determine the relevant subjective values and preferences, your conscious perspective as an agent rationally assessing and then choosing which future to try to bring into actuality is thwarted, for you cannot use this perspective to determine which acts maximize your expected subjective value. And this means you cannot use the normative rational standard as a guide for first personal decision-making. The implicit assumption of decision theory was that, as long as we could describe the outcomes, we had the information we needed to assign the relevant values and determine our preferences. But in first personal decision-making involving transformative experience, this assumption fails.

Transformative experiences, then, confront you with the basic unknowability of your subjective future in a context where new and dramatic changes are occurring, and transformative decision-making draws out the consequences of that epistemic fact. In an important sense, when facing a transformative choice, you lack the knowledge you need in order to have authority and control over who you will become when you choose how to act.[5] You can't navigate these decisions by stepping back, rationally evaluating your different subjective possibilities, and then choosing the act that maximizes the expected subjective values of your future lived experience. That is, when faced with such choices, you *can't* clear-sightedly map your possible futures out and first-personally assess them to guide your life course, rationally evolving your perspective forward and updating as you go. Instead, you grope forward in deep subjective ignorance of what your future conscious life will be like.

Even where the transition is gradual, so that you can rationally evolve your point of view forward through the immediate future, you may have very little epistemic access to what it will be like to be you after an extended temporal period. The depth of the subjective poverty involved in transformative choice can come out when you reflect on a past experience and realize just how little you knew beforehand about

---

[5] As I noted in chapter 2, we do not face this problem for choices that do not require us to imaginatively assess the possible outcomes. I know all the outcomes of stepping in front of a bus are bad, and so I won't do it. I don't need to assess the outcomes by envisioning them to make my decision. So I set these kinds of cases aside, as I have throughout the text.

what it would be like to undergo it. (Consider how little you knew, say, ten years ago, about what it would be like to be you right now.)

Parents engage in these sorts of reflections all the time. They love to talk about how little they knew before becoming a parent. Perhaps they knew that they'd cradle their newborn in their arms, they'd feel her soft skin and smell a distinctive baby smell—and more generally, that they'd love her unselfishly, and that they'd have many sleepless nights with her—but they didn't know what it would be like to hold and love their very own baby, or to undergo these experiences as a parent, with all the love and concern the attachment to one's child brings, or how dramatically their preferences about their lives would change. Reflecting back on one's career choices can bring out the same kind of rueful reflections. For example, a person who has chosen to become a surgeon working in the trauma unit of the ER might have known, in some sense, that he'd face life and death situations involving real human beings. But before he worked in the ER, he didn't know what it would be like to actually undergo experiences like attempting—but failing—to save the life of another human being, or how he'd respond to such experiences.[6]

As a result, we should come to terms with the fact that our lives as we really live them, as individuals with first personal perspectives on the world, are just not lived as a series of events where, from whatever particular point we are at in our lives, we know how we are determining our subjective future selves. Certain kinds of experiences simply have to be lived before we can know what we need and want to know about them.

If we leave things like this, then we should conclude that the ideal of self-realization through choice and control of our subjective futures, understood in terms of knowledgably mapping out and selecting

---

[6] Your own death is the ultimate transformative experience, and as such, you are particularly ill-equipped to approach it rationally. This doesn't mean it can't be rationally chosen. You can rationally choose to permanently end your experience, and then rationally choose to do this by way of death.

possible futures for ourselves, is a chimera. And so we should conclude that we cannot use the normative rational standard, a standard that embeds requirements that we cannot meet from our first personal perspective, as a guide for living. The natural and appealing notion of living your life by regularly engaging in a process of reflective deliberation, considering a range of acts with various possible outcomes, and choosing the acts that best realize your hopes and preferences for your future, cannot be rational in the way we prereflectively thought it could be.

We find ourselves in a Sartrean dilemma: when making transformative choices, either choose authentically, or choose rationally.

A fan of standard decision theory might want to respond by claiming that we should drop this silly, romantic view of authenticity based on choosing from a first personal perspective. Edit out the first person, and choose rationally from the third personal perspective, always prioritizing the agent's preferences at the (tenselessly understood) time of the choice.

I find such a response unappealing in the extreme. I agree that we need to preserve some version of decision theory. But doing so by dismissing the first personal view on decision-making is a kind of disownment of the value of one's own consciousness. The value of reflective assessment and choosing and planning our subjective futures comes partly because we think about who and what we are and who and what we want to become. We, each of us, have a sense of what we want to become through our choices, in the sense that we know what we want our subjective selves and subjective future preferences to be. To live life in a meaningful way requires us to reflect on our life's choices and to choose from our personal perspective, in a way that is consistent with our best moral, legal, and empirical standards, but is also consistent with our subjective preferences about the nature of our conscious future experiences, and allows us to knowingly choose in accordance with those preferences. We want to determine how we evolve over time by owning and guiding our subjective futures.

If we want to preserve authenticity along with rationality, then, we need to reassess the way we are thinking of how to make these decisions from the first personal perspective, and by extension, we need to think about how to reformulate the structure of the decision model.

There might be room for optimism here. Recall the recommendation for a reconfiguration of the decision to try a durian for the first time: instead of constructing the decision in terms of whether you will enjoy the taste of durian or whether you will find it revolting, you should decide to try durian solely for the sake of having the experience, good or bad. The subjective value attached to the outcome of trying durian reflects the subjective value of gaining information about the nature of the experience, not whether the experience is enjoyable or whether it is unpleasant.

In other words, if we change the structure of the choice about durian, we can fit it to normative decision models after all. Instead of constructing the decision in terms of whether you will enjoy the taste of durian or whether you will find it revolting, you can choose to try durian based on whether you want to have a new experience for its own sake, that is, solely for the sake of the value of having the experience, whether what it's like to have that experience is subjectively good or bad. That is, you decide to try a durian for the sake of the revelation the experience of tasting a new kind of fruit brings.

The relevant outcomes, then, of the decision to have a durian are *discovering the taste of durian* versus *avoiding the discovery of the taste of durian*, and the values attached reflect the subjective value of making (or avoiding) this discovery, not whether the experience is enjoyable or unpleasant. If you reconfigure the decision this way, your choice can be framed as a choice of whether to try something new solely for the sake of having the experience that is, for the sake of the revelation it brings.

The advantage of reconfiguring your decision this way is that, on the assumption that you can assign subjective values to having new experiences for the sake of discovering them, it allows you to use normative decision-theoretic models to represent the structure of the decision-making process and guide your choices. If you have had epistemically transformative experiences in the past, you can draw on what you know from such experiences to determine, for you, the subjective value of having epistemically transformative experiences. Since normative decision theory does indeed capture a way we should reason reflectively about our subjective futures if we want to reason rationally (maximizing expected value is the way to go!), and since choosing rationally is preferable to not choosing rationally, this type of reconfiguration represents an important alternative strategy to use when dealing with choices involving epistemically transformative experiences that are made from the first personal perspective.

If the response to epistemically transformative choices like trying durian is to reconfigure the decision to focus it on the value of discovery, this suggests a way to respond to transformative choices more generally. Return to the case of choosing whether to become a vampire.

Unlike the durian case, the stakes in the vampire case are high. How you make the choice will have deep, significant, and lasting effects on your future. Choosing to try a new experience just for the sake of discovering it seems just fine if all you are risking is the possibility of an unpleasant breakfast. Choosing to make a discovery that entails risking life as you know it is an entirely different sort of proposal.

In a high stakes case it is even more important to find a way to meet the normative standard. Following our durian solution, we might try recasting the case, changing it from a consideration of outcomes such as *what it will be like to be a vampire* to considering outcomes such as *discovering what it is like to be a vampire* versus *not discovering what it is like to be a vampire*, where the subjective values are of discovering or not discovering what it is like to have this kind of experience. If you reconfigure the decision this way, you reframe your choice of whether to become a vampire as a choice of whether to have the experience for its own sake, that is, if you choose to do it, you choose to do it for the sake of discovering what the experience of being a vampire is like.

To configure this decision to make it rational, we need to keep in mind, again, that the values of these outcomes are *not* determined by whether the experience involved is good or bad, but solely by the sub-jective value of the discovery of the nature of the experience, what-ever it is like. The decision of whether to become a vampire could then be framed as a decision based on the value of discovering the vampire experience: we'd act for the sake of discovering the nature of this radi-cally new experience.

In this case, however, the sort of revelation we'd be interested in wouldn't just be the sort of information we gain from having a brief, new experience like trying a durian or seeing a new color. Instead, we'd be interested in the sort of revelation that comes from experiencing a new way of living our lives, that is, from experiencing what it would be like to live life as a vampire. The sort of revelation involved, then, isn't merely sensory, but rather the kind of revelation we discussed at the end of chapter 3, where we explored the idea that there was revela-tion involved in discovering life as a parent that is not represented by the standard interpretations of the empirical work on well-being and parenthood.[7]

If we want to act for the sake of this sort of revelation, the revela-tion associated with lived experience, and if we have the right kind of previous experience with making radically new discoveries about our lives, perhaps we could assign positive subjective value to the revela-tory experience of discovering what it's like to live life as a vampire.

But this response, while on the right track, is too quick, because the revelatory experience of becoming a vampire also changes your core personal preferences, making you into a different kind of conscious being.

---

[7] The value of lived experience, even experience involving suffering, is brought out very nicely by Havi Carel's work on the phenomenology of living with chronic illness, especially when that illness is episodic, allowing one to recover for periods of time. That is, if one can recover for long enough to respond to the illness by building and forming a lived perspective, one achieves some-thing of value, the value of "learning to live well within physical and mental con-straints" (Carel 2014a).

If becoming a vampire was not a radically new kind of experience for you, you could simulate forward by, in a sense, mentally putting yourself in the shoes of the person who had become a vampire and evaluating the outcome from that perspective. But since you don't know how the change will be wrought in you (because you don't know what it will be like to become a vampire), you don't know which new core preferences you'll have. In other words, you won't know whose shoes to mentally step into to assess the values of the post-change outcome.[8]

In chapter 2, an analogous fact created a problem for our reformulation of the decision in the microchip case, where we confronted a choice between discovering a new kind of sensory ability versus keeping the ability to taste. In the microchip case, the problem arises because of the transformative nature of gaining a new sense modality while losing another. In such a case, core preferences involving sensory experiences and their effects will be revised, but we don't know how they will be revised. And this means that we cannot assume our relevant preferences will remain constant in our decision model, nor can we know how our preferences will evolve. In particular, a person's preferences about the subjective value of revelation involving sensory capacities could change in virtue of having the revelation itself. For all the agent knows, her pre-experience self could place a low value on discovery, while her post-experience self could place a high value on it. Or vice-versa. Given the transformative nature of the situation, before having the experience, she cannot reliably project forward to determine whether and how the preference change will occur in her.

So there are two levels to your vampire decision. First, you cannot determine the expected subjective value of the lived experience of being a vampire by simulating forward and imaginatively representing outcomes in terms of what it's like to be vampire, because you haven't had the right kind of experience. Second, you cannot simply choose between

---

[8] There are obvious personal identity questions in the background for the pre-experience self who is choosing to become the post-experience self.

which preferences you'd prefer to have, human or vampire, because the nature of the change is such that you don't know what your vampire preferences will be.

Because you cannot compare the different preferences in order to apply a higher order preference ranking to choose between them, you find yourself without a decision rule in this situation. The standard approach would be, then, to assign priority to your current (human) preferences, since it is your current self who is making the choice. But as we saw in chapter 2, it isn't clear that this is the right thing to do. For after all, you might have evidence, via testimony, that new vampires are almost always extremely happy with their decision to become a vampire. So it might seem that you should prioritize the preferences you'd have as a vampire. Maybe when you face the choice of whether to become a vampire, given the radical preference change that is likely to attend the transformation, you shouldn't avoid becoming a vampire based on your current human preference for, say, remaining vegetarian, because you are ignoring the preferences of the self who you'd become if you decided to become a vampire.

We saw the very same issue arise in chapter 3, when we considered the choice to have a child. Here, the prospective parent who places a high value on remaining child-free faces an even worse dilemma, because, while friends and relatives tend to testify to their satisfaction after becoming parents, the empirical work suggests that well-being plummets. In this case, the evidence from testimony of friends and relatives suggests that the reluctant prospective parent should prioritize the preferences she'd have after becoming a parent, whereas the scientific evidence suggests she should prioritize the preferences she has before becoming a parent. The problem, then, is that there is no clearly correct decision-theoretic rule about which set of preferences to prefer at this level: those of the current, decision-making, child-free self or those of the future self who has become a parent.

In these situations, then, you are faced with making a choice between discovering the outcome of having an experience where you transformatively change, adopting new (and unknown) personal preferences and having a wide range of new kinds of experiences, and the outcome where you avoid making this discovery, keeping your original preferences and experiences much the same as before.

How, then, are you to choose?

Perhaps revelation can still save us—it's just that we must push the level higher. If you choose to have the transformative experience, to choose rationally, you must prefer to discover whether and how your preferences will change.[9] If you choose to avoid the transformative experience, to choose rationally, you must prefer not to discover whether and how your preferences will change.

The idea is that if you choose revelation, you choose it for its own sake. The revelation involved in discovering what it's like to be a vampire isn't just a discovery about, say, what it's like to glide around elegantly as a vampire in a fashionable black cloak. It's a revelation that involves discovering how you respond to the transformation of becoming a vampire, which includes discovering how your preferences evolve in response to the transformative experience. If you choose to become a vampire, you choose a new kind of life, where you become a new kind of person (vampires are people too, they are just nonhuman people). You choose, then, the revelation involved in discovering what it is like to live life as a different kind of being, and by extension to discover whatever core preferences you'll end up having. The choice you are facing is the choice between discovering who

---

[9] What if your preferences to discover whether you'll have new preferences change as the result of the transformation? At t1, you are choosing to discover how your preferences evolve at t2, but when they evolve at t2, they evolve so that you no longer prefer to discover how your preferences evolve. One version of this problem is easily avoided by temporal indexing: at t2, your preferences about evolving preferences would concern how your preferences would evolve from t2 to t3. But we can also make sense of a change such that, at t2, you have evolved so that your post-change you, at t2, prefers that at t1, you wouldn't prefer to discover how your preferences evolve at t2. This is still consistent, however, because at t1 you preferred to discover whether and how your preferences would change, and at t2 you discovered that your preferences changed so that you preferred that you had not had such preferences at t1.

you'd be as a vampire versus keeping your life the same way it is. You choose to discover a new identity with its new preferences, or you choose to retain your current identity and current preferences.

Similarly, the decision to have a child could be understood as a decision to discover a radically new way of living with correspondingly new preferences, whether your subjective well-being increases or not. On this account, if you choose to have a child, your choice is to discover the new experiences and new preferences of a parent, whatever they will be. You decide to have the experiences of life as a parent, with all its up and downs, its happiness and sadness, and its changes in what you care about (perhaps you are motivated by the fact that many people think it is a kind of experience that defines an important way to live one's life). So when you choose to become a parent, you choose to become a certain type of person and to live your life a certain way, but you don't choose it because you know what it will be like—you choose it in order to *discover who you'll become*. When making this choice, all you really have to guide you, apart from any previous experience of the subjective value of revelation, are general facts, such the fact that you'll have less time, money, and energy to pursue other activities, the fact that after having a child, parents report feeling happy with their choice, and the fact that if you have a child, your core preferences will almost certainly undergo some sort of significant change.

Or, if you choose to be childfree, you choose to forgo a revelation of a certain type. You don't know what it would be like to have a child, but you are not choosing on that basis. You are choosing based on the fact that you don't want to create and satisfy the new preferences you'd have as a parent. You are happy with the current preferences you have, your preferences to pursue other experiences that you find valuable, such as travel, exciting career opportunities, and an unfettered life. Perhaps you feel this way because you enjoy your life as it is now and think the kinds of experiences you are having now (and want to continue to have in the future) are characteristic of a well-lived life. When you choose to avoid becoming a parent, you choose to be a certain type of person and to live your life a certain way, but you don't choose this because you know what it is like to be a parent—you choose it *because you reject this kind of revelation*—you don't want to discover the new preferences and new identity that comes with becoming a parent. Such a discovery, for you, holds no appeal.

In either case, when choosing to have a child or choosing to remain childless, if you choose rationally, you choose on the basis of whether you want to discover new experiences and preferences or whether you want to forgo such a discovery. You choose whether you want revelation, or whether you don't. It is a decision that may be viewed as constituting an opportunity, one that carries value in virtue of the value of discovering what the experience of living life as a parent involves, or conversely, as an option best left unexplored.

In general, then, the proposed solution is that, if you are to meet the normative rational standard in cases of transformative choice, you must choose to have or to avoid transformative experiences based largely on revelation: you decide whether you want to discover how your life will unfold given the new type of experience. If you choose to undergo a transformative experience and its outcomes, you choose the experience for the sake of discovery itself, even if this entails a future that involves stress, suffering, or pain.

Mistakes will be made. But a well-recognized feature of what it means to live an authentic, deliberative life is to learn how to live with the effects of one's choices for oneself: authentic living partly involves the discovery of what it is like to choose and respond to events in one's life. Even if your choices bring about hardship or reduced well-being, they are not without revelation, for there is revelation involved in what it is like to experience the consequences and evolved preferences resulting from one's acts, and there is revelation associated with living up to and managing those consequences.

Whatever transformative decision we are considering, taking the revelation involved to the level of preferences about preference change, as opposed to trying to decide based on the character of the particular subjective values of the lived experiences involved, allows us to follow the normative standard and embrace a decision-theoretic rule to prioritize the preferences of the current, decision-making self. On such a basis, we can choose rationally, as long as we are guided by revelation, and are careful not to let illicit, unjustified assumptions about what it will actually be like to be a vampire (or to be a parent, or to have a new sense ability, or to be a doctor, and so on) infect our decision procedure.

This might seem like an appealing way to resolve our dilemma. The trouble is, for some people, it won't be at all satisfactory. Why not? Because if we have to choose to have a transformative experience on the basis of preference revelation, that is, by preferring to discover the preferences we'd develop, then we must prefer to give up any current first-order preferences that conflict with the new preferences we'll end up with. Many of these first-order preferences may be preferences that we think of, in some way, as defining our true selves.[10]

If, for example, you choose to become a vampire, adopting the higher-order preference to evolve your preferences in whatever way they would evolve when you became a vampire, then, once bitten, if your preferences evolve toward bloodlust, you have to give up any first-order preference for being vegetarian. Or perhaps, as a human, you value working with disadvantaged children. If you choose to become a vampire, you commit to the possibility that your preferences evolve into valuing cold selfishness and cultivating spiders, and you no longer have any interest in helping disadvantaged children. And so on: if you choose to become a vampire, almost any of your first order, self-defining preferences could be up for grabs.

Similarly, perhaps you choose to become a parent, consciously adopting the higher-order preference to evolve your preferences in whatever way they will evolve when you have a child. Once you become a parent, your preferences might evolve so that you no longer prefer to write books, travel to exotic locations, climb mountains, go out dancing on the weekends, or stay late at the office. That is, once you become a parent, your preferences may evolve in a way that makes you

[10] For related discussion, see Derek Parfit's (1984, p. 327) example of the nineteenth century Russian nobleman.

into a different kind of person, a person who embraces a new life with a very different way of living. If so, then when you choose to become a parent by adopting the higher-order preference to evolve your preferences, you are deciding that you no longer value these first-order preferences as much as you value discovering the new preferences.

The problem is that most of us have first-order preferences that conflict with how our preferences could evolve, and we might take some of these first-order preferences to be essential or self-defining. But to rationally choose to undergo a transformative experience, we must give these first-order preferences up. And while we might want to be able to meet the normative standard for decision-making when facing important life decisions, this is a heavy cost to bear for doing so.

Understanding the structure of the decision in this light suggests that there is something to our Sartrean dilemma after all. The situation is not that we cannot make big life choices rationally, nor that rational agents cannot choose from the first personal perspective. The dilemma is, instead, that in a case of transformative personal choice, we can either attempt to meet the rational standard by choosing based on either avoiding or embracing revelation, or we must find some way to justify the way we intuitively want to use our first-order preferences and imaginative, first-order assessments to guide our reasoning and deliberation about the future.

My conclusion, then, is that something has to give.

In such cases, which include many real-life contexts where we simply do not have epistemic access to the subjective values of our future lived experiences, I argue that we should choose rationality plus revelation. We must embrace the epistemic fact that, in real-life cases of making major life decisions in transformative contexts, we have very little to go on. To the extent that our choice depends on our subjective preferences, we choose between the alternatives of discovering what it is like to have the new preferences and experiences involved, or keeping the status quo.[11]

---

[11] This, then, is different from the moral version of the Sartrean puzzle where you must choose between two different outcomes, each of which has a moral

If we decide to choose this way, when facing big life choices, the main thing we are choosing is whether to discover a new way of living: life as a parent, or life as a hearing person, or life as a neuro-surgeon, and so forth; that is, we choose to become the kind of person—without knowing what that will be like—that these experiences will make us into.

Or, because we value our current preferences more highly than we value the (mere) discovery of new ones, we reject revelation. That is, we refuse to renounce our first-order preferences, choosing instead to retain the ability to taste, or to keep a child-free life, or to remain Deaf.

In choices between transformative experiences, where keeping the status quo is not an option, for example, a forced choice between a career as a violinist and a career as a doctor, we must discover what it is like to live one type of life rather than another type, perhaps by picking between equally revelatory options.[12]

The lesson of transformative experience, then, is that if you want to choose rationally, you are forced to face your future like Marlow, in Conrad's *Heart of Darkness*, as he sails along the coast of Africa. "Watching a coast as it slips by the ship is like thinking about an enigma. There it is before you—smiling, frowning, inviting, grand, mean, insipid, or savage, and always mute with an air of whispering, 'Come and find out.'"[13]

When faced with each of life's transformative choices, you must ask yourself: do I plunge into the unknown jungle of a new self? Or do I stay on the ship?

claim on you. This is not the sort of choice where we are primarily choosing between, say, the moral duty of caring for our ailing mother and doing our patri-otic duty.

[12] Perhaps we can only pick a career, not choose a career, in the sense of "pick-ing" developed by Ullmann-Margalit and Morgenbesser (1977).

[13] I'm indebted to Joshua Rothman for calling my attention to Conrad's novel in his discussion of my work on transformative experience in the *New Yorker*, "The impossible decision" (April 23, 2013).

# AFTERWORD:
# DECISION-MAKING

The central argument of this book is that the epistemically and personally transformative nature of transformative experience creates problems for an individual-level decision procedure based on cognitively modeling or envisioning outcomes of acts involving these experiences.

My argument raises more questions than it answers, and I have been fortunate to receive a wide range of responses to it. In this Afterword, I would like to engage with some of the many excellent comments and criticisms raised by my interlocutors, without assuming that I have engaged with all of the dimensions of this issue that one could explore.

Below, I will discuss how problems with transformative experience connect with first personal choosing, counterfactuals, limitations on empirical projections, informed consent, rational addiction, indeterminate utility, imprecise credences, higher-order computational modeling, and models for unaware agents.

## First Personal Choosing

I've been framing big decisions like whether to have a child or whether to become a doctor in very subjective terms, insisting that we think about them as decisions made from the first personal point of view. Although objective moral and social and other factors are relevant to our assessment of decision-making, they have not been the primary focus of my discussion. I set these considerations aside not because objective values are not relevant to any well-considered and thorough deliberation, but because I wish to isolate and critique the distinctively first personal element of our choices.

Big life decisions concerning our subjective futures are most naturally framed, at least in part, as decisions made from the first personal point of view, where we mentally model different possible types of lived experiences for ourselves and then choose between them. These decisions are ordinarily understood as involving, in an ineliminable way, judgments about what our subjective futures will be like if we choose to undergo the experiences involved in the decision to act. When moral and other values are represented first-personally as psychological reasons for making a choice, they can also be represented in the subjective values we assign.

We could argue that we should simply eliminate the first personal, psychological stance we take when making a choice. But such a reformulation requires us to substantially revise our ordinary way of thinking about such decisions.[1] In effect, we'd have to give up our autonomy in order to preserve our rationality.

As I've made clear, the problem of transformative decision-making is *not* based on the idea that decisions cannot involve considerations drawn from third personal sources such as objective moral considerations, or empirical work in the social and behavioral sciences, when possible choices and outcomes are being evaluated.

Of course we can consult these impersonal sources when assessing alternatives. The worry is not that we cannot or should not do this. Rather, the worry is that, by eliminating the first personal psychological stance, normative constraints on our decision theory would effectively imply that, in contexts of transformative choice, *no* first personal preferences based on "what it's like" considerations can play a central role in the evaluative process. And this is a disaster, for while we are happy to consider moral rules or scientific data when making big and important decisions in our lives, as individuals facing our life's choices, we are not—and should not, for practical as well as

---

[1] Gilbert (2007); Wilson (2011); and Kahneman (2013) do an excellent job of showing that revisions are needed in any case. See Haybron (2012) for an interesting and skeptical view of our ability to assess our past and present affective states.

principled reasons—be happy to simply ignore or eliminate our subjective perspective from its central place in personal decision-making.

There are two kinds of reasons why, when you are making a big decision about your subjective future, you need to make it in a way that retains first personal, psychological assessment. (Given the solution I proposed in chapter 4, if your decision is transformative, the first personal, psychological approach you should take involves assessing the desirability of revelation.)

The first kind of reason for a first-personal assessment is practical. Sometimes there just isn't complete guidance from the impersonal sources: for example, the moral and legal rules may not have much to say about whether you should get the microchip that replaces your sense of taste with a new sensory ability. Or sometimes the morally right thing for you to do depends on first personal considerations, such as considerations concerning what you think it'd be like for your child to be able to hear in a species-typical way. Empirical guidance can also be incomplete. This was brought out in the discussion of the vampire case in chapter 2 by the supposition that the study of vampire psychology is in its infancy. The practical empirical constraint derives from the fact that, when making many actual decisions in the real world, we can't make a big decision about our subjective futures based solely on what experts about psychology, behavior, neuroscience, and society tell us about how people generally respond to making certain types of decisions, because we don't have enough of the right kind of information to predict how we, as individuals, will respond. There are practical limitations on empirical data. (The next section, on the fundamental identification problem, discusses this in more detail.)

A common situation to find yourself in is a decision situation where you know, at least roughly, what the relevant outcomes might be, but you don't know enough about which outcome you'll be most likely to experience, or about how you'll respond to the outcome that actually occurs. You won't know this, because the scientific information you have isn't personalized enough to make accurate individual-level predictions. The science just hasn't developed enough yet. For example, empirical research, at least in the near future, isn't going to exhaustively *determine* whether you should decide to have retinal surgery or not, or whether you'd prefer being a violinist to being a doctor. This is related to what is often called the "reference class problem." In low-stakes cases, the reference class problem can be ignored. But in high-stakes cases, cases where your life or way of living is at stake, it prevents you from casually replacing your first personal evaluations with empirical data.

If we had individual-level data that could tell us how likely a particular outcome was for us and how we'd respond to it, then we could argue that big life choices should be made in the same way that we choose not to step in front of a bus or to be eaten by sharks. In cases like the bus or the sharks, we don't need to perform an assessment of the outcome by cognitively modeling what it would be like, because we know what the results would be: we know every outcome is bad, whatever it is like. If empirical work could simply describe the results that were causally determined by our individual-level properties, along with how satisfied we'd be with them, we might be able to simply replace our ordinary deliberative procedure with the expected values specified by these results. In effect, we could turn our personal decision over to the experts. But for the sorts of big life choices I've been focusing on, we don't have sufficiently detailed data to do this, and it's not clear we ever will.

The second kind of reason to preserve a role for the first-personal perspective in decision-making is principled. When we make big decisions about our futures, we want to think carefully about them. This is why normative decision theory matters to us: we are planning out our personal futures and the futures of those who depend upon us, and we want to do it as rationally as possible. But we also want to choose authentically, that is, we want to choose in a way that is true to ourselves, in a way that involves our *self* as a reflective, deliberating person. It is natural to think of our point of view and our subjective perspective on the future as a defining feature of who we are, where we have control and authority over who we are by making choices that determine what our futures will be like.

Perhaps you disagree. If first personal assessment creates problems, why not get rid of it? At least in principle, if the data existed, we could replace our first personal perspective with empirical facts and eliminate the role for subjective values and preferences. Or, if the moral rules are known, we can simply use those to determine the decision. Why shouldn't we see such replacement as the truly rational response?

It is important to see how performing this replacement would do great violence to our ordinary way of thinking about deliberation. Again, my argument is not that we cannot consult moral, empirical, and legal sources for guidance, or that we cannot attempt to influence our first personal perspectives using these kinds of sources. Indeed, I hold that when we value first-personal revelation and choose experiences in order to see how our preferences will evolve, we should make such choices in concert with our best moral, legal, and empirical standards.

My argument is, instead, that we should not replace our first personal deliberation with what is, in effect, a program that applies an empirically determined or morally determined behavioral algorithm to our decisions, so that as agents faced with decisions, we merely feed in an initial possibility and wait for the computer or the scientist (or the philosopher) to tell us how to act.

As individuals facing personal life choices, as real people making decisions about our futures, we don't just want to know what others tell us about the probabilities and values of outcomes, or to have the computation of the outcome determined independently of our personal inclinations. We want to know what *we* think and what *we* care about. This is one reason it seems wrong to insist that, to be rational, individuals must make decisions about their future subjective perspectives based solely on third personal considerations such as moral or environmental considerations, at least, when it is given that the lives of others are not at stake and that what is at issue are individuals' own subjective futures. The same point holds when we consider decisions made on the advice of experts. Just as there are many cases in which you should not be rationally obligated to make personal decisions solely on the basis of moral and social and other factors, it is unclear whether you can be rationally obligated to make personal decisions solely on the basis of the empirical data, where this entails replacing your opinion with the expert opinion of others.

If, to be rational, you must determine your subjective values from third personal data alone, you must give up your privileged perspective, the conscious point of view that defines your mental self. If you are forced to give up your first personal view, you're forced to deliberate in a way that implies your preferences determined by your first personal assessment of your possible future experiences don't matter to your rational calculation.

Recall the bizarre idea from chapter 3 that Sally, who has always wanted to have a child, should ignore her personal values and preferences when she chooses. After reading the empirical data and expert (majority) opinion that suggests having a child lowers subjective well-being, she decides to ignore her personal preferences and remain childless.[2] Or consider Sam, who hates the sight of blood, avoids hard work whenever possible and has no interest in medicine, yet decides to become a surgeon simply because he knows it is a morally valuable thing for him to do. This way of making decisions seems wrong from our ordinary perspective, because it seems to violate normative rules for deliberating carefully and thoughtfully about how you should choose to live your life.

[2] As Christia Mercer pointed out to me, US society places significant responsibility on the individual who is making the choice. It's not like we're living in a communal society where the responsibilities of childcare are shared: the heavy burdens we lay on the shoulders of parents makes it even more important that individuals think about their preferences for their futures, given that they are the ones who are expected to take on the vast majority of the responsibilities involved. If the response to my argument is that we should be expected to eliminate considerations of our experience when we make big life choices, then the structure of social support needs to change so that responsibility for those choices is no longer an individual matter. Telling someone that they should have a child for reasons of loyalty or society or science and then abandoning them to their future is not an appealing moral or political position.

A further problem with leaving your subjective perspective out of your decisions connects to the Sartrean point that making choices authentically and responsibly requires you to make them from your first personal perspective.[3] A way to put this point is that if we eliminate the first personal perspective from our choice, we give up on authentically owning the decision, because we give up on making the decision for ourselves. We give up our authenticity if we don't take our own reasons, values, and motives into account when we choose. To be forced to give up the first person perspective in order to be rational would mean that we were forced to engage in a form of self-denial in order to be rational agents. We would face a future determined by Big Data or Big Morality rather than by personal deliberation and authentic choice.[4]

Perhaps because we value the privileged perspective each of us has on our own self from our conscious point of view, we want to consider our own subjective preferences and attitudes from our first personal point of view and choose from that perspective (Moran 2001). If we don't choose this way, then in an important sense, we alienate ourselves from our choices, and thus alienate ourselves from our own futures. In other words, if you don't make choices about your future from your own personal point of view, and instead step back and attempt to map out choices based only on some sort of impartial, uncommitted, third personal point of view, you in effect cede authority over yourself.

This holds in two senses. It holds if you disregard your personal point of view entirely. But it also holds if you merely build in your personal point of view as though you were some kind of impartial observer, that is, if you attempt to make a decision by combining third personal empirical information with a third personal stance towards the first personal view of the decision-maker, where that decision-maker just happens to be yourself.[5] Neither stance is appropriate for authentic,

---

[3] Moran (2001, p. 164).

[4] Susan Wolf's (1982) "Moral saints" brings out related issues.

[5] Moran emphasizes that we shouldn't take a third personal view on our first personal view. We must *occupy* our first personal view when we deliberate.

responsible decision-making, for neither stance incorporates the kind of first personal commitment each of us makes when taking control of our lives and realizing the effects of our own decisions.

I must admit that one possible conclusion to draw from my arguments in the main text is that individual decision-makers should, in fact, cede authority to science. After all, science is a guide to truth, and there are those who will be less concerned to preserve first personal deliberation than I. But if this is the conclusion, it needs closer philosophical scrutiny and criticism. If, to be truly rational, we must give up the first personal stance, then meeting the normative rational standard is costly indeed.

## The Fundamental Identification Problem

In the previous section, I argued that, for practical reasons, we should not simply replace personal-level psychological assessments of high-stakes outcomes with empirical data from the social and behavioral sciences. This section explains the methodological underpinning for the practical concern.[6]

Empirical disciplines such as psychology, economics, and sociology collect data on large groups, and subdivide these groups based on externally determined criteria, giving us information about how different types of people tend to respond to different experiences. The research is often focused on broad demographic categories, for example, on what people of different socioeconomic classes, genders, races, and cultures tend to do, often with further subdivisions based on general characteristics like age, health, background, life stage, leisure pursuits, personal abilities, and personality traits. Such information is extremely useful at the impersonal or social level for decision-making, for example, for the development of public or institutional policies, or for the assessment of cultural or economic trends. But from the personal point of view, when an individual is making decisions for herself, this information is, at best,

---

[6] I am particularly indebted to Kieran Healy for discussion.

only partially useful. This is because the data just do not give us the kind of fine-grained information about how a person who is just like us, a person with just our particular blend of personal abilities and personality traits, our likes and dislikes, our work ethic and neuroses, and so forth, is most likely to respond to a particular experience.[7]

Individuals are complex entities, each person has a distinctive psychological profile and background, and so may respond to an event in a unique way. This means that, even in the same context, different people can have very different personal psychological reactions to having the same type of experience, depending on their individual blend of psychological properties and capacities, even if, when surveying large groups, trends correlated to general characteristics emerge.[8] As a result, when a person is making a decision for herself about her future, she cannot simply substitute social-scientific findings for her own subjective perspective and expect to get a satisfactory result. When it comes to our own choices, the only sufficiently fine-grained guide we actually have to construct our predictions about how we respond to experience is our own self-knowledge and our detailed grasp of our personal point of view.

Of course, we can combine our self-knowledge with coarse-grained empirical information to inform and give us guidance. We can use the two kinds of information together, but we cannot *replace* our fine-grained, subjective perspective with predictions from empirical data without far more fine-graining than contemporary science gives us. When considering whether to undergo an experience of a particular type, unless you know just what type of person you are, and which type you fall under that is relevant to the context of concern, and, moreover, that all or virtually all people of this type respond in the same way to having the sort

---

[7] And complicating all of this, of course, are possibilities like the one we explored in the vampire case, where an individual's preferences are changed by undergoing the intervention (recall the vegetarian neighbor who loves being a vampire now that she's become one).

[8] I am setting aside physiological reactions, which, when the relevant data exist, admit of more precise prediction and assessment.

of experience you are considering, empirical results are not sufficient to guide you perfectly to the values for the experiential outcomes you should expect. The problem, in essence, is one of self-location: we don't know enough about the fine-grained details to know which group of respondents we will end up in.[9] One way to try to fill the gap between impersonal data and the personal perspective is to introspect to the possible results. That is, when confronted with a major personal decision, to close the gap between the impersonal and the personal, the individual uses the data in conjunction with imaginative introspection to assess her personal responses to different treatments or outcomes. The implicit recognition of the need to close the gap may be a reason that informed consent is given such a central role in public policies designed for individuals (for more, see the section on informed consent).

The insufficiently fine-grained nature of empirical information is a version of a well-known problem for social scientists, the *fundamental identification problem*. The fundamental identification problem arises from the fact that the ideal measure of how a given event at time $t$ will affect an individual would involve a comparison of the actual individual after she is affected, at time $t+1$, to the counterfactual, unaffected version of herself at time $t+1$:

> The fundamental problem in program evaluation is that it is impossible to directly observe outcome gains for the same person in both states. To deal with this issue, some classical approaches focus only on identifying mean treatment parameters and rely on conditional independence assumptions to solve the selection problem. Matching has become very popular in this field . . .[10]

The issue here is that the same person can never be simultaneously observed in different "treatment states," that is, we cannot observe both the actual outcome and the counterfactual outcome of an event acting on a particular individual. Obviously, the problem is that

---

[9] Again, it's related to the reference class problem.
[10] Heckman, Lopes, and Piatek (2014, p. 38).

counterfactual outcomes are hard to measure empirically: we can't just go to unactualized possible worlds and gather the data.

In other words, scientists certainly collect individual level data in the sense that characteristics are observed at the level of individuals. But the fundamental identification problem makes it clear that it is not possible to collect data in the *truly* individual sense that we want when, as individuals, we face our big life choices. The best social scientists can do is evaluate individuals as members of groups with certain identifying characteristics, and compare members of the group who undergo the event to members of the group who do not.

There are various sophisticated ways that contemporary social scientists approach the problem of finding and comparing relevantly matching individuals. The general idea is to try and find the best actual world counterparts for the target group. For example, if the research question involves the effect of living in a poor neighborhood, sociologists may compare an individual living in a poor neighborhood to an individual living in a wealthier neighborhood, where these individuals are as similar as possible with regard to as many characteristics as possible, as long as these characteristics are independent of properties one has as the result of living in a neighborhood with a particular economic status. The idea is that, if the individuals are as similar as possible in the relevant sense, then by pairing them and observing their different trajectories over time, the effect of living in a poor neighborhood is measurable by comparing differences between the properties of the individuals over time. In effect, the premise is that the similarities between the individuals will minimize the possibility of error due to undetected but relevant differences between the individuals. However, while matching similar individuals is an effective research tool, and may be the best strategy available, it and other quasi-experimental methods obviously cannot eliminate the fundamental identification problem.[11]

---

[11]  As Jeremy Freese pointedly observed: if the matched individuals are so similar when they start out, then why is one person living in a poor neighborhood while the other is not?

The fundamental identification problem derives from the physical fact that empirical information for decision-making in types of actual-world situations can only be developed using comparisons of *different* individuals, with different physical and psychological profiles. It brings out why empirical science relies on assessments at the level of groups rather than at the level of any particular individual, and why projections for individuals are constructed from this group-level data. Such projections are based on detectable, measurable, third personal features of individuals who are members of the groups, and sophisticated measures are developed to correct, as far as possible, for relevant differences between individuals within the groups.

The methods used by social scientists are powerful and increasingly sensitive to basic problems of causal inference. They are successful enough when it comes to social policy that it can be tempting to elide the technical worries raised by the semantics for counterfactuals, the reference class problem, and the demands of the normative standard for rationality. But the perspective taken in the empirical literature is very different from the subjective perspective of the individual, who, in personal situations, when making a big decision for herself, has to try to judge, from her first personal psychological perspective, what *her own* responses would be.

As the problems raised by transformative experience bring out, these perspectives can be in tension when policy knowledge meets individual choice at the level of personal decision-making. An individual who faces a life-defining transformative choice is interested in how *she* could be affected by a particular event, not how someone who is merely similar to her is actually affected by that event. And so, since she cares about *her own* actual and counterfactual responses, she measures them, as best she can, by projecting forward into her psychological future and modeling her possible responses to the event in question. This is the deep methodological basis for the practical limits on an individual's replacing her personal perspective with the empirical perspective. Such a replacement will always bring the risk that the social-scientific data she is relying on is too coarse-grained for a decision made at the level of the individual.

And here is why, in the context of transformative choice, a special problem arises. In ordinary decision contexts, if enough empirical data is available, imaginative assessments based on projections concerning one's individual response to treatment might allow the individual to close the gap opened up by the fundamental identification problem. Closing the gap between actual and counterfactual by imaginatively assessing possibilities is a useful and important strategy in ordinary contexts where we have to determine how, as individuals, to make use of impersonal data. But in contexts of transformative choice, such projections are not justified—an individual cannot close the gap by imaginatively assessing her different possible personal responses to different events. Introspection about how she, personally, is likely to respond cannot help her, because of the epistemic inaccessibility of the nature of the transformative experience. Yet transformative contexts are precisely those for which it is most important to be able to close the gap, since transformative decisions involve the possibility of major life changes, and so are extremely important. This is just the context in which you most want to rely on your ability to imaginatively project forward and assess the way that you, as a particular individual, will respond to the transformative event—but you cannot do so, at least, not in a rationally justified way. And so, when real individuals in real situations face transformative choices, the abstract and seemingly practically irrelevant questions raised by the fundamental identification problem shift their ground and come into focus as related to central, practical, and pressing concerns that each of us must tackle in life-defining contexts.

## Informed Consent

Imagine facing the following choice.[12] You've been healthy and physically active all your life, with no disabilities or chronic pain. However, just as you retire and start considering Florida real estate, you discover that you need an operation to save your life. Your surgeon tells

---

[12]  I am indebted to Kieran Healy for discussion.

you that if the operation is unsuccessful you will die, but if the operation is successful you can expect to have a normal lifespan.

You decide to have the operation, but there are further details you need to take into account. In particular, you have to choose between having the operation using a new technique or having the operation using the standard, tried-and-true technique. You know all the available medical facts: your surgeon is the best available, he has performed the new technique with a 30 percent success rate, and if the operation using the new technique is successful you will be pain-free and without any permanent disability. A 30 percent success rate isn't great though. The trouble is, even while your surgeon has a 97 percent success rate using the old technique, a successful operation using that technique will leave you with chronic, severe pain and disability. You have only one chance to have the operation, because it involves surgery that will permanently damage the organ involved.

How do you decide which technique to have? One option is to allow your surgeon to tell you how to choose. But since it is *your* life and death that hang in the balance, you feel that you should make the decision, now that the surgeon has given you all of the information that medical expertise can supply. After all, how he would tolerate chronic pain might be very different from how you'd tolerate chronic pain.

Your first task is to value the outcomes, and your outstanding problem is to assign subjective value to the outcome of having permanent, chronic pain and disability.[13] The obvious problem is that what crucially matters is how you think you'll respond to living that way, that is, what it would be like for you to live with this pain and disability. For if, for you, living with chronic pain and disability is as bad as, or even worse than, death, then you should choose to have the operation with the new technique. But if living with permanent pain and disability is better then dying, then depending on the details of how difficult it would be for you

---

[13] For simplicity, I am assuming that complicating factors such as wanting to stay alive so as to keep your pension paycheck coming, or allowing yourself to die so that your spouse receives a hefty insurance payout, are not present.

to live that way, you might want to choose to have the operation using the old technique.

What is knowable in this situation, and what isn't? How, as an informed patient, are you supposed to make this decision? How are you supposed to decide on which technique you want your surgeon to use?

The question embeds the problem of transformative choice into a context of informed consent. What do we take ourselves to be doing with such consent? The basic idea is that you, as the patient, are supposed to evaluate the different outcomes, determine their values along with the level of risk you can tolerate as a result, and control the decision-making on that basis. But, crucially, then you need to know *how you think you'll respond* to different possible experiential outcomes.[14]

And in this context, you are unable to get the information you'd need. The problem, of course, is that there is good reason to think that you, with your history, cannot assess the subjective value of living the remainder of your life with severe pain and disability, or know how your preferences could evolve given your different possible experiences in the different

---

[14] Data about how others who have had the operation respond to living with chronic pain and disability won't always help the patient who is attempting to decide whether to have the operation, for patients attempting to make an informed choice face a version of the reference class problem along with the fundamental identification problem. That is, how do they know which similarity matters, given all the different classes of respondents that they are similar to in different ways? Which of the classes that they belong to is the *relevant* class that they should locate themselves in? In order to use empirical results to guide your decision at the individual level, you have to know which group of subjects you are most similar to in the relevant respects, that is, you have to be able to locate yourself in the right reference class. But, given the radical changes in experience that result from having the operation, how can you know which reference class you belong in unless you already know how you will respond to being in chronic pain and being disabled? As Alan Hájek (2007) has argued, this problem is just a version of the problem of discovering the right prior probability distribution over the relevant hypotheses. The connection of the problem with the priors to the decision-theoretic issues of non-forecastable preference change that I raised in the main text should be clear.

possible scenarios. If you cannot determine your values and considered preferences for the outcomes, you cannot rationally determine the act with the highest expected value. The point generalizes, of course, and raises the question: what are we doing when we give our informed consent? What is the individual capacity that is being exercised here that makes a patient's informed consent important and worthwhile?

The structure of this case is relevantly similar to the case of a parent deciding whether her child should receive a cochlear implant, or to a case where, say, a blind saxophonist is choosing to have retinal surgery, and even to a case where a person is choosing to have a child. If, in such cases, we cannot determine the expected value of the act, why think that an "informed" consent is doing what it is supposed to do, that is, why think that the agent is really being given the opportunity to make a choice while being informed in the relevant way? In some cases, such as those involving medical procedures, giving up autonomy and letting the experts decide might be the only thing one can do. But when making choices such as whether to try to get pregnant, whether to terminate a pregnancy, or whether to choose cochlear implant surgery for your infant, giving up autonomy is an untenable option. If the justification of informed consent is rooted in a person's ability to understand her values and preferences concerning different possible outcomes, transformative choices pose a serious challenge.[15]

As I noted, there may be some reason for a patient to want to voluntarily give up autonomy when faced with medical decisions involving uncertain outcomes. There are also related questions about how to understand patient decision-making and autonomy in the sociological literature. As work on the exchange of human blood and organs shows, there is a way of understanding the role of informed consent as a practice designed to give patients the *mere impression* of rational agency and control over the outcomes, a practice that can even involve encouraging patients to visualize or imagine fictional outcomes of

---

[15] For an interesting and controversial discussion of informed consent, see Levy (2014).

their decisions in order to suggest a way of subjectively valuing them. The reason for encouraging patients to envision fictitious outcomes is that patients who make their choices under the impression that they have a sense of what the outcomes will be like, even if the sense is grounded in purely fictitious "facts," may in fact respond better to the actual outcomes, however they turn out.[16] In other words, an implicit recognition of our epistemic inability to evaluate transformative experiences may be subtly embedded in certain deeply practical strategies involved in managing the psychological framing of patient decisions and organ exchange.

## Rational Addiction

My reflections relate to discussions of rational addiction,[17] along with ideas about "pre-commitment devices" and future discounting.[18] If a potential addict can't know what it will be like to have the high that could get him addicted, how can he, in principle, rationally choose to become addicted, or rationally choose to avoid addiction?

Standard models of rational addiction assume that the potential addict has fixed and unchanging preferences over his lifetime consumption patterns. He can predict with perfect foresight how his preferences at a given time in the future will change as a result of his choices today. If the potential addict knows that he'd prefer having the preferences of the addict to his current preferences, he can compare his options. But if this feature of the model is removed, in certain contexts, the problem of transformative decision-making arises. In such cases, the key fact is that without the knowledge of what it will be like to enjoy the high so

---

[16] Healy (2006). Healy's work in this area focuses on the procurement strategies involved in human blood and organ exchange. He notes that "this might suggest that organizations manage donors as ants tend to aphids, farming them assiduously and stroking them for nectar as needed. But individual expectations and organizational capacities have coevolved" (p. 113).

[17] I'm indebted to John Quiggin for discussion.

[18] See Elster (1979), Elster (1997), and Becker (1998) for discussion.

much that you desperately want it to continue, the addict cannot make the comparison between his pre-hit self and his post-hit self.

And, indeed, we can imagine a case involving a drug that affects people in variable ways. Ninety-nine percent of those who try it do not get addicted with the first hit. But 1 percent do. In other words, this drug is so powerful that, for those of you among the unlucky 1 percent, once you experience the high, you have an intense and overwhelming desire for *more*, and you don't care about anything else. All you want is to experience that burning, bright, intensely beautiful high.

Now imagine someone who has never used this drug, but who really wants to try it. He just wants to have one hit to see what it's like. (He wants to know what all the fuss is about.) He has never experienced the kind of intense high that this drug provides—indeed, that's part of the attraction. Perhaps he's had experience with a wide range of other drugs, and never got addicted or even felt the need to try them more than once. So he thinks that he can handle a bit of experimentation, that is, given his previous experience, he thinks he won't get addicted with the first hit.

The trouble is, that until he experiences the particular, gripping, and distinctive kind of high that this drug gives, he cannot know how intensely it will affect him. He has to have the experience of this kind of high in order to be able to judge whether it is so intense that he will become addicted. But, once he knows how it will affect him, it will be too late. The problem is not just one of uncertainty, it's one where the agent is unable to grasp the relevant content. Like ordinary Mary in her black-and-white room, he is not able to know what the experience is like, but since what the experience of the high is like will determine his future preferences, it is not possible for him to know his future preferences without having the experience.

As it turns out, once he takes his first hit, he experiences a pure and intense longing for another hit, a longing like nothing else he's ever experienced. While the high lasts, he cares for nothing more but continuing the high itself, and as it fades, he is seized with the desire for more, and will do anything to get it. If his new preference structure remains, that is, if he is in fact addicted, then he is the victim of a transformative choice: he acted rationally given his pre-addiction preferences to have only one hit (just to see what it was like), but the high changed his preferences in a way that he could not foresee.

We don't have to try very hard to imagine such a drug: the popular perception of crack cocaine is of a drug that is so powerful that some people can get addicted the first time they use it.

## Indeterminate Values

Recent work by Alan Hájek and Harris Nover (2004, 2006), develops a case based on a gamble they call the *Pasadena game*, and argues that this is a case where we cannot assign an expected value to playing the game. In the Pasadena game, because of the way the game is structured, the expected utility, that is, the expected value, is indeterminate, leading Hájek and Nover to conclude that a value cannot be assigned to playing the game.[19]

The result is related to well-known decision-theoretic puzzles with cases like the *St Petersburg game* in which the expected value of playing the game is infinite. In that game, a fair coin is tossed until it comes up heads, and you receive exponentially escalating payoffs. The longer it takes to get heads, the higher the payoff, and since the increase in payoff is exponential, the payoff increases rapidly. To calculate the expected value of the game, you sum the probabilistically weighted values for each of the possible outcomes and get the mathematical result that the expected value of playing the game is infinitely high.

The problem the St. Petersburg game raises for expected utility theory is that, if the expected value of playing the game is infinite, standard theory seems to tell us that you should be willing to pay everything you've got (assuming your worth is finite) just to play the game once. This seems wrong, and raises questions about the ability

[19] I am indebted to Alan Hájek, Andy Egan, and Kenny Easwaran for discussion.

of standard decision theory to handle cases involving infinitely valued outcomes, at least when it is thought of as providing the normatively rational standard for making decisions where agents start with assigned values and probabilities and then calculate expected utility results.

The Pasadena game is different from the St. Petersburg game, but raises a related problem. In the Pasadena game, according to Hájek and Nover, the expected value of playing the game is not infinite; rather, the value is mathematically indeterminate. In this game, a coin is tossed until it comes up heads, the possible payoffs grow without bound, and the payoff for the first time the coin comes up heads alternates: positive values (rewards) alternate with negative values (costs). The indeterminacy comes from the peculiar structure of the Pasadena game, for, as it turns out, the expected value of playing it depends on the ordering of the payoff table: depending on how the alternating terms of the payoff are rearranged, the expected value of any particular play can be infinite, or if the terms are rearranged, it can diverge all the way to negative infinity. Hájek and Nover conclude that the value of playing the game is mathematically indeterminate, and the upshot, on their view "is that there is no fact of the matter of how good the Pasadena game is, at least in terms of expected utility, and hence in terms of standard decision theory" (Hájek and Nover 2006, p. 705).

Hájek and Nover conclude that the Pasadena game and its variants pose a deep threat to standard decision theory, where standard decision theory is understood as an approach to rational decision-making where agents start with values (or utilities) and probabilities in order to evaluate choices.

Now, Hájek and Nover's conclusion is controversial, since it depends on accepting that the game itself is coherent. Critics have suggested alternative approaches.[20]

---

[20]  Colyvan (2006); and Fine (2008). Kenny Easwaran (2008) argues that there are intuitive reasons to value the Pasadena game using its weak expectation. This

But whether or not the game is actually coherent, I draw the lesson that *if* the game is coherent, and *if* its expected value is indeterminate or unassignable, then standard decision theory faces a problem. If there exist coherent games with indeterminate expected values, either standard decision theory cannot handle such games and needs to be revised in order to handle them, or there is nothing to be said about how good such games are.[21]

Why do games matter? Because decision theorists use games to model decision problems and the strategies we should use to rationally approach them. So, the conditional lesson from the Pasadena game should be generalized: if there is a decision problem with indeterminate expected values, either standard decision theory cannot handle such a decision and needs to be revised in order to handle it, or there is nothing to be said about how rational the decision is.

You might think this is all just fun and games. That is, you might think these games are interesting and fun to think about, but that there is no relevant structural similarity to cases we actually care about: these games just concern esoteric mathematic possibilities generated by complex rules and artificial contexts. They aren't something that agents making personal decisions would ever confront.

means that there are at least some ways of playing the Pasadena game that give a determinate, very low expected value (less than a dollar!), suggesting that there is hope for standard decision theory in some contexts. Since there is no parallel expectation for cases of epistemic transformation, solving the decision theoretic problem for transformative choices requires some other strategy.

[21] To the extent that decision theory gives us guides for rational action, where such guidelines are modeled by playing various sorts of games, this result raises important questions about the ability of decision theory to handle cases with indeterminate expected utilities. If we are confronted with structure in some decision-theoretic context that is relevantly similar to the structure of such games, it would seem that, without significant modifications, decision theory cannot be used to make a rational decision. That is, there is no rational way to make sense of playing a game with that structure, and so no rational way to maximize expected value in a decision case with that structure.

But, in fact, the nonmathematical cases we've been discussing, like the case of choosing to try durian or the case of choosing to become a vampire, share an important similarity with these games. In particular, cases of decision-making involving transformative experiences can share the same deeply problematic feature that, in the Pasadena game, gives the undesirable result: the expected values are indeterminate.

Recall the description of subjective decision-making from chapter 2, where you engage in a kind of cognitive modeling from the subjective perspective. To make a choice, you construct a mental model of the situation, thinking of the different options, running a mental simulation of what it would be like, and assigning it a subjective value based on what it would be like. You then assess and compare these values to make your choice.

Transformative experiences throw a wrench into this process, because they are epistemically transformative. If an option involves an epistemically transformative experience, you lack the parameters you need to run the simulation for that option. So if you can't run the simulation, because you can't know what it is like, then you can't assign it a value.

Consider the *durian game*: you are visiting Thailand for the first time, and need to choose between having a piece of ripe pineapple and having a ripe durian for breakfast. You've never eaten a durian, nor anything resembling it. To play the game, you have to choose and eat a fruit for breakfast. To win, you have to choose the kind of fruit that you'd like the most. So you have to choose between having pineapple and skipping durian, or having durian and skipping pineapple. If you choose pineapple, and it tastes better than the durian would taste, you win. If you choose pineapple, and it tastes worse than the durian would taste, you lose. If you choose durian, and it tastes better than the pineapple would taste, you win. If you choose durian, and it tastes worse than the pineapple would taste, you lose.

It should be obvious that, unless you know what it would be like for you to taste a durian, that you cannot play this game if you want to choose based on what you think the taste will be like. Until you taste a durian, you have no idea whether you'll like durian more or less than pineapple. The upshot is that, if you don't know what it is like to taste a durian, there is no fact of the matter of how good the durian game is for you, at least in terms of expected value, and hence in terms of standard decision theory.

Now we can tweak the game a little bit: imagine the value of winning the game is tied to the intensity of your pleasure in eating the fruit, and the cost of losing the game is tied to the intensity of your disgust in eating the fruit. This makes the game more complicated, because, in principle, you can win big or win small, and lose big or lose small. If you choose pineapple, and it tastes much better than a durian would taste, you win big. How big? It depends on how much better, relative to the durian, the pineapple tastes. On the other hand, if you choose the pineapple and it tastes only a little better than the durian would taste, you win small. If you choose pineapple, and it tastes much worse than the durian would have tasted, you lose big. If you choose the durian, and it tastes much better than pineapple would taste, you win big, and so on.

When faced with a durian game whose values are tied to the relative degree of pleasure or disgust you experience with the relevant outcomes, it becomes clear how ineffective decision-theoretic models are for cases like this. For not only are you unable to judge whether or not you should play the game, for any outcome that requires a comparison of the taste of durian with something else, you can't judge what its value is, nor can you judge its relative value. So for any such outcome, if you have never tasted durian, you cannot rationally assign that outcome a value—that is, for any such outcome, its value is epistemically indeterminate.

We find ourselves with the very same problem we had when considering the Pasadena game. No model of decision is available to the game-player who chooses based on what she thinks it will be like to taste durian, for, just as in the Pasadena game, she cannot determine the expected value of playing the game. This is particularly apt when thinking of rational choice in terms of credences, subjective values, and epistemic utility theory. If the agent cannot determine the expected value of playing the game, standard models of epistemic utility don't apply. Or, put another way, they fall silent on the value of the game.

The basis for the similarity between this feature of the Pasadena game and cases of epistemically transformative experience has nothing to do with the mathematics of infinitely valued outcomes. Rather, it's because both cases put the decision-maker in a position of epistemic indeterminacy. The mathematical indeterminacy of the value of the Pasadena game leads directly to epistemic indeterminacy: it entails that there is no way to rationally assign a value to playing the game. In decisions involving epistemic transformative experience, the facts about experience entail that, given the way the decision is structured, the values of the relevant outcomes are epistemically indeterminate. The source of the epistemic indeterminacy comes from the nature of experience-based knowledge rather than mathematical indeterminacy, but it is the fact of epistemic indeterminacy itself that matters, not where it comes from. The decision-theoretic implications are the same.

Consider, now, the *baby game*: you've never had a child. To play the game, you have to choose whether to have a child. To win, you have to choose the act with the results that you'd like the most. So you have to choose between having a child and passing up the joys of a childfree life, or having a childfree life and passing up the joys of being a parent. If you choose to have a child, and being a parent has a higher subjective value than living the childfree life, you win. If you choose to have a child, and being a parent has a lower subjective value than living the childfree life, you lose. If you choose the childfree life, and being childfree has a higher subjective value than being a parent, you win. If you choose the childfree life, and being childfree has a lower subjective value than being a parent, you lose.

But unless you know what it would be like for you to have a child, you cannot rationally play this game, because you cannot rationally value the outcomes. And here, given the personally transformative nature of the experience, you cannot even model how your values and preferences would change if you played the game one way (having a child) versus playing it another way (remaining childfree). The upshot is that there is no fact of the matter of how good the baby game is, at least in terms of expected subjective value.

The consequence of all this is that if we wish to preserve decisions such as whether or not to have a child (or to become a violinist, or to try a new drug, or to get a cochlear implant, and so on) in the way in which I have been framing them, as subjectively based decisions necessarily involving considerations of the character of one's subjective future, either decision theory understood as expected value theory needs to be revised, or it must be limited to the decision problems it can fit—or, as I have argued in this book, *we need to change the way we play the game.*

## Finkish Preferences

The Pasadena game connects with the first part of the problem with transformative choice, the epistemic problem of subjectively valuing outcomes. The second problem of transformative experience, the fact that having the experience changes your personal preferences, connects with well-known puzzles involving dispositions.[22]

If an experience is personally transformative, and you know how it will personally transform you, you can know how to simulate your different possible lived experiences and assign them values in a way that accommodates your future preferences, even before you have the experience that changes you.

But when the experience is, at once, both epistemically and personally transformative, you can't predict what simulations you will need to run, since your parameters change in virtue of having the experience itself, and you can't know how you'll be changed until you have the experience. Having the experience of performing the act and its immediate consequences can change your assessment of the expected value of your act, so until you have the relevant experience,

[22] I am indebted to Richard Pettigrew, Matt Kotzen, and John Collins for discussion.

you don't know which simulations you'd need to run (or how you will value them).

The point is that you, as a cognitive simulator of possible outcomes, are *finkish*.[23] A finkish simulator is a simulator whose original disposition to simulate disappears when it undergoes the experience: it changes its disposition just when the experience is had. As a finkish simulator, you change how you simulate when you are put to the experience. You have preferences about your possible future as a vampire, and those stay the same, so long as you are not bitten. But when you are bitten, because what and how you value changes, how you'd simulate changes, and thus your preferences change.

The problem here, of course, is that you are supposed to perform a simulation in order to decide whether to have the experience in the first place. But because you are finkish, before you have the experience you should perform one kind of simulation, because of the kind of preferences you have at that time. But when you have the experience, you change, such that the simulation you should have performed is different. And you only change your preferences *because* you were put to the experience: it is the experience itself that brings about the change. That is: you have finkish preferences.

Now, add to the finkishness the fact that you can't know how you will fink. As I discussed in chapter 2, because you don't know what it will be like to have the experience, you can't employ higher-order techniques to try and simulate the new and different outcomes and their values that would determine your post-experience preferences. You can't, as it were, before you've had the experience, put yourself in the shoes of the post-experience person (you after the experience) and run those outcomes, because you can't know what values that post-experience-you will assign. In other words, in this sort of case, you are transformatively finkish.

---

[23] "A finkishly fragile thing is fragile, sure enough, so long as it is not struck. But if it were struck, it would straight away cease to be fragile, and it would not break" (Lewis 1997, p. 144).

So, if the experience is epistemically and personally transformative, you, as the simulator, are in decision-theoretic trouble, because you are a finkish simulator. When you face a transformative choice, then, you face the fact that you are a *transformatively finkish simulator*. If an agent has transformatively finkish preferences, then, she cannot satisfy van Fraassen's (1984) Principle of Reflection.[24]

## Imprecise Credences

Instead of reformulating transformative choices in terms of revelation, could we respond by relaxing the normative standard for decision-making?[25] We already have independent reasons to think the normative standard needs changing, because we have reasons to think that cases where we don't have precise credences need special treatment.[26] Perhaps the real problem with transformative choices are that they are members of a class of decisions involving imprecise credences.

Let's look at this using the example of choosing to have a child. Here, you are choosing whether or not to have a child, basing your decision on whether you'd prefer to become a parent or whether you'd prefer to live your life childfree. The suggestion above is to understand this transformative choice as a problem stemming from the agent's inability to assign precise credences. So, for example, the suggested interpretation for understanding the epistemic difficulty you face before you have your first child is that it is due to the fact that you simply don't have enough evidence to warrant any particular assignment of

---

[24] Fraassen (1984). According to van Fraassen, rationality requires that your credence in proposition $P$ at t1 is your current expectation of your credence in $P$ at t2.

[25] I am indebted to Richard Pettigrew for discussion.

[26] There is no standardly accepted approach, and there are two main proposals that are hotly debated: (i) whether we need imprecise credences at all, and (ii) whether they create problems for decision-making, for example, by making us vulnerable to money pumps. See White (2009); Elga (2010); Joyce (2010); Moss (forthcoming); Carr (n.d.).

credences to the states needed to bring about the range of outcomes associated with having a child. Put slightly differently, the problem is framed as a problem where, when facing the choice, we find ourselves faced with a range of possible subjective values associated with having a child, and we don't know which credences to assign to the states of the world needed for the outcomes in this range.

Understood this way, the problem about choosing to have a child comes from epistemic ambiguity concerning which act will maximize expected value, since acts are functions from states to outcomes, and you don't know which credences go with which states. If so, various decision-theoretic models have been proposed for this situation. In particular, the right response to the lack of evidence you have about what it will be like to have a child might be to think of your doxastic state as modeled by a *set* of probability assignments to states and their corresponding outcomes, rather than by a single probability measure over the possible states.

In other words, perhaps the problem is that, in one frame of mind, you think that you know the subjective value of what it's like to have a child is very high, say, when you are imagining yourself joyfully cradling a cooing newborn, and you believe an outcome with a high subjective value has a reasonably good chance of obtaining, given your current credences. So you assign credences such that having a child maximizes your expected subjective value. But in the dead of night, you find yourself in a different frame of mind. Perhaps you imagine a constantly screaming, colicky child, and the relentless drudgery of changing diapers, combined with months of sleepless nights, or perhaps you dread outcomes where you have a disabled child, such as a child with Down Syndrome or a child with dwarfism. . . and then assign credences such that remaining childless maximizes your expected subjective value.[27]

And so on, such that you have a set of different ways of assigning credences to states of the world, where these different ways of assigning credences result in different, conflicting ways of maximizing your

[27] Moss (2015).

expected subjective value. Perhaps the problem with determining what it is like to have a child is really this one: we simply don't know which way of assigning credences is the right one, and the evidence we have is not enough to warrant assigning *any* particular assignment of credences. So your set of ways to assign credences must include many, many possible way of assigning them.

If you *could* actually know what the different subjective values were for your different possible outcomes, this would be an interesting way to model the situation you'd be in. Once you were justified in assigning subjective values to the different possible outcomes of what it would be like for you to have a child, you'd have the subsequent problem of determining which credences to attach to which states of the world, and it is plausible that this problem would involve issues with imprecise credences. And, in fact, some people who have not had a child do seem to think about the problem this way, that is, they agonize over which way they should assign their credences in order to decide what to do.

If this were our situation when we face the choice of whether to have a child, I still think we'd be in pretty deep and rather interesting trouble, especially because this is such a central, life-defining decision that people want to be able to face rationally—and there is no consensus about how to handle imprecise credences. But this is *not* the situation, at least not in the first instance. For, as I've argued above, you *don't* actually know what the different subjective values will be for your different possible outcomes. How you will value the outcomes is determined by what it is like for you to generate and stand in the attachment relation to your child. Moreover, until you know what it is like to have your child, you can't even know the *range* of the subjective values. That is, you don't know just how wonderful it could be to have your particular child, and all the experiences that follow from this, or just how awful, or heart-wrenching, it could be (if, for example, your child is born severely disabled, in great pain, with only a few months to live). How bad, or how good, could it be? Possibly *very* bad, or possibly *very* good—but that's about all you know. You don't even know if the range of outcomes is symmetrical, that is, that whether the best possible outcome is as high on the scale as the worst possible outcome is low. Perhaps the value of the worst possible outcome is very, very bad, while the value of the best possible outcome is merely good, or quite good. Moreover, as I discussed in the main text, because generating and standing in the attachment relation to your child changes your preferences, this calls into question *any* model of your decision that is based only on the preferences of your pre-experience self.

The main problem, then, is the same problem we had in chapter 2, when we discussed the possibility of becoming a vampire, or the possibility of having a chip implanted in your brain that would eliminate your sense of taste while endowing you with a new sensory ability that is stunningly different from the usual five. In the sensory capacity case, you must choose to discover a new kind of sensory ability in place of the ability to taste, or you choose to retain the ability to taste instead of discovering a new kind of sensory ability. The problem here is that you can't compare having the new sense ability to what it is like for you to have the sense of taste in order to decide which one you'd prefer. You can't even make a decision based on comparing the range of the values of having the new sensory ability to the range of values of tasting things, because without actually knowing what it is like to have the new sensory ability, there isn't any useful sense in which you can know the range of the values of having it. And finally, you face the central problem of transformative choice: that you don't know how having these new sensory experiences could change your preferences.

That is, knowing what it is like to have a new sensory ability by actually deploying the sensory ability in experience is precisely what determines your judgment of how subjectively valuable, from your point of view, it is to have it, and is what would give you the ability to predict how it would change your preferences. By extension, knowing what it is like to have the new sensory ability by actually deploying the sensory ability is necessary for you to know whether you want to trade in your ability to taste. The experience of having a new sense is simply too radically different from your previous experiences, and too potentially life-changing, for you to be able to assess the subjective value of having it and the way your preferences could evolve before you know what it is like.

Like the experience of gaining an entirely new sensory ability, you must experience what it is like to have your child before you can know the range of subjective values involved, how to compare the subjective values, and what your new preferences might be.[28] If you don't know the subjective values of your outcomes, or the range of values, or how your preferences will evolve, then decision-theoretic models for imprecise credences are of no use, for the problem, at least in the first instance, is with knowing the subjective values and how to handle the change in preferences, not with assigning degrees of subjective belief.

But does this mean we are completely stuck here? Are the tools from formal epistemology of no use at all? Let's step back and look at the choice to have a child again, and see where formal epistemology can take us.

Is there anything we know about the situation that we can exploit to make progress on the problem of transformative choice? Before having the transformative experience, we don't know the individual subjective values of the outcomes, we don't know the range of these values, we don't know how to compare them, and we don't know how to predict our preference change. But let's assume we do know, in our case of choosing to have a child, that the possible outcomes could be very good, or very bad, or something in between. So even if we don't know exactly what the range is or how to compare the values, we know the values are possibly very positive or very negative and (we assume) they are comparable.

What this means is that small changes in information can have big effects, because knowing even a little bit more about a high-value outcome can have a significant effect on calculations of expected value. Even a little bit of information about the values of these outcomes or the

---

[28] Andrew Solomon's (2013) gives an excellent account of how the preferences of parents with disabled children can evolve.

credences we should attach to them could result in a significant change in expected subjective value.

For example, if you were able to find out that the range of the values was asymmetric, such that the worst outcomes were very bad, while the best outcomes were merely pretty good, and you were also able to discover the respects in which they were comparable, then if you adopted a rule that current preferences were to receive priority, you could exploit a version of the models for decision under ignorance that we discussed in chapter 2. In such a situation, you would be rationally permitted to choose to remain childless, because the asymmetric shape of the value space is so heavily tilted towards the negative.

On the other hand, if you knew that, perhaps because of the psychological changes that having a child wreaks in a parent, that the range of the subjective values was asymmetrically tilted towards the positive, and you adopted a rule that post-experience preferences were to receive priority (and relied on the testimony of satisfied friends and relatives), perhaps you could be rationally permitted to choose to have a child merely on this basis.[29]

Do we have this information about the shape of the value space? In particular, can we exploit the psychological facts about preference change (setting aside, for the moment, the worry about whether we can rationally choose to change our preferences this way) to know that, whatever it is really like to have a child, we will find intense, revelatory, positive subjective value in it, and so the negative outcomes are minimized? Or, on the other hand, can we know that the worst outcomes are very bad, but the best outcomes are only pretty good?

No. And the reason, again, stems from the basis for the cognitive phenomenology of having a child, which derives in part from the attachment formed between the parent and child. Forming this attachment is part of the ground for the revelatory nature of the

---

[29] I'm making a lot of big assumptions here about the legitimacy of adopting the decision rules about preferences, relying on testimony, and so on. But it's worth seeing how far we could go under such assumptions, even if I don't think it will pan out in the end.

experience, and also for the change in preferences that parents experience. A direct consequence of forming this attachment, and the revision of preferences it entails, is a new and deep emotional vulnerability, one which allows for a wide span of subjective values.

Once she exists, you care very much about your child, and about what happens to her. And in particular, given the attachment you form to your child, if she is born severely disabled such that she experiences great pain and suffering, or dies in infancy, you will experience an indescribable amount of emotional and psychological distress. The specter of the suffering and death of one's child engages a parent's greatest fears. Anecdotally, parents report feeling an intense joy, rating having a child as one of the most rewarding experiences of their lives. But the intensity of the love for one's child brings a vulnerability that can also come with great costs.

This strongly suggests that either there are no exploitable asymmetries, or that we don't know enough about the nature and shape of the value space to rationally choose to have a child based on what it would be like. If you had more information about what it would be like for you to have your child, you might be able to determine enough about the value space to find a useful asymmetry and to determine how your preferences would evolve. Once you had this information, if you had even a small amount of information about how you should assign credences to the states needed for the different subjective outcomes, you might be able to use this to determine any significant asymmetry in the expected values of your acts. When the stakes are high, even a small asymmetry in probability can be significant. But in most real-life cases, you don't have what you need to get started.

We might put it this way: the main problem with truly transformative choices is not a problem in formal epistemology; it is a problem in formal phenomenology. To make a start on the problem, we need to think about the possibility of developing models for epistemically indeterminate values, perhaps starting by examining ways to model imprecise values (although since the real problem is the special kind of epistemic inaccessibility of the values, models for imprecise values won't be able to do all the work). Imprecise credences, at least in the first instance, are not the problem, although if we solve the formal phenomenology problem we'll still need to address the assignment of imprecise credences and give an account of how to manage temporally evolving preferences in transformative contexts.

So it is not rational, when deliberating about parenthood, to agonize over which probability distribution over the known subjective outcomes you prefer in your set of probability assignments, because at this stage you don't even know the subjective values of the outcomes, and so you don't know which assignments of probabilities should be in your set and which should be excluded, and finally, you don't know what your new preferences will be if you undergo the change.[30]

That said, it would be rational to agonize and deliberate if agonizing would give you information about which values you should assign to subjective outcomes. What sort of information would we be trying to discover by such agonizing? We'd be trying to discover what sorts of experience-based information we might already have available to us, given our previous experiences, to use in simulating the outcomes involving the new experiences of parenthood and assigning them subjective, phenomenal values.

The kind of evidence we'd need is not evidence that summarizes testimony or statistical facts about well-being. What we need is evidence that could tell us about which higher-order phenomenological features of the experience of what it's like to have a child are shared by experiences that prospective parents have already had or could have before making the decision to have a child. Such experiences are not experiences like changing a diaper.[31] They would have to be experiences that

[30] So the case is not analogous to the rational indecision described in Moss's (2015).

[31] They might include caring for the children of others, but only if something about experiencing the attachment you'd form to these children was relevantly like the experience of the one you'd form with your own child—and the only reliable way to know whether this is the case is through collecting empirical information about such shared experiential character.

were able to teach you something about what it is like to be attached to your newborn, with all of its attendant emotion, vulnerability, stress, and excitement. This raises an interesting possibility. Perhaps the sort of experiences you'd need to have to grasp partial information about what it's like to have a child does not need to have anything (first-order) to do with children at all. The relevant experiences just need to share the right higher-order phenomenological character.

This is where empirical psychological work could contribute key insights. One important way empirical work could be of help is in collecting further testimony from parents and nonparents to try to determine the range and symmetry or asymmetry of possible subjective values. But a potentially more interesting and valuable approach could be modeled on the idea developed in the next section, that, to make progress on puzzles involving transformative experience, we might be able to exploit hierarchical Bayesian modeling techniques to uncover shared higher-order phenomenological characters, for example, between concepts had by congenitally blind subjects and concepts had by sighted subjects. If research in cognitive science could uncover shared higher-order phenomenological characters between experiences had by non-parents and experiences had by parents, this information could be used by prospective parents to try and model features of the relevant outcomes to determine partial subjective values. If you could get partial information about the value of what it would be like to have a child, you could use this to determine facts about the value space, to help you get a sense of how your preferences might change, and perhaps to determine which models, if any, for decision under ignorance could employed to make a rational choice.

What about credences? Here, again, empirical work can be of use. Once you have information about the subjective values of the outcomes, even partial information, you can use it to determine *something* about what your credences should be, even if what you determine suggests only a slight shift in probability assignments, or only excludes a few probability assignments from your set of options. As I noted above, even a slight shift in credences in a high-stakes case might be enough to help us rationally choose how to act, and if we could combine this information with models for value imprecision, I see the potential for getting some traction here. This is where agonizing about the decision might make more sense.

So what is key is discovering what sort of cognitive information is relevant, that is, discovering, through empirical work, which parts of a person's previous experience, understood from her subjective point of view, could be exploited to give her the information or the ability she needs to determine the contours of what it is like. Such information would be higher-order in the sense that it would be knowledge of relevantly similar or isomorphic features of her previous experiences that she could then use to cognitively model, or at least cognitively guide and constrain, her assessment of the relevant subjective values of her possible future experiences. In the next section, I will discuss this in more detail.

## Hierarchical Bayesian Models

Imagine a case where a congenitally blind adult must decide whether to have retinal surgery in order to be able to see. Such an adult, let us assume, has built his life around his blindness, choosing a career (he is a saxophone player, whose soulful music reflects his lived experience and his highly trained auditory capacities) and a way of living and understanding the world through touch and sound, a way of living that is deeply tied to his blindness.

Should he have the surgery? To decide, he would need to find a way around the epistemic wall created by the transformative nature of the choice, one that preserves a role for his first personal perspective in evaluating and assessing his subjective values and evolving preferences. Is there such a way? There might be.[32] Instead of simply

[32] The connection that I sketch in this section between transformative decision-making and hierarchical Bayesian modeling was suggested to me by Josh Tenenbaum. I am indebted to him for very helpful discussion about the ideas developed in this section, in particular, for discussion about higher-order structure and the role of Bayesian models in learning and planning, and for further discussion about the adaptive value of discovery.

eliminating the first personal perspective from decision-making and attempting to replace it with third personal testimony or descriptions, perhaps he could use empirical work to help him leverage knowledge from his previous experience to construct a partial phenomenological guide to the possibilities the surgery raises for his subjective future.

The idea for how to do this comes from work in cognitive science on learning and representation. This work explores how humans can make accurate and flexible predictions about novel situations using inductive inferences that draw on abstract or higher-order similarities between situations they've already experienced and novel ones they haven't. The models use probabilistic frameworks to provide explanations of learning and generalization in terms of Bayesian inferences. They exploit the fact that our cognitive phenomenology represents the world in a range of different ways, and part of that representation involves an experience of the world as having a certain kind of structure. We use our experience of the structural form of the world to organize and guide our first personal understanding of future experiences, by using our previous experience of the relevant higher-order categories of the world to make predictions about our responses to new situations organized by those same categories.

Consider the choice to try a new species of grape. Assume that you've had lots of grapes of different kinds before, and in general, you are a big fan of grapes. They taste good. Should you try the new, bright orange grapes at the farmer's market? It seems like you should, reasoning that, in the past, you've liked red grapes, green grapes, blue grapes, and black grapes, that is, you've liked grapes of different colors, so you have liked grapes in general. While you like and appreciate the distinctive flavors of each different type, you also really like *grapes*, that is, you like this type of fruit along with liking the different instances of each subtype. Liking a type of fruit, grapes, can be understood as liking something that all of the different subtypes of grapes have in common. They share certain features, that is, they are similar in certain respects to each other. This sharing can be understood as sharing a universal, *grapehood*, or, equivalently for our purposes, as sharing a kind of abstract or higher-order categorical structure. Your experience leads to you think that you like things in the *grape* category.

When you reason that you'd like the new kind of grapes because you've liked grapes in the past, and so you decide to try the new grapes, you can make the decision by assessing the subjective value of eating grapes. To assess the subjective value, you evolve your first personal perspective forward to the outcome where you taste the new grapes, imaginatively constructing an outcome where the orange grapes have the same tasty properties as grapes you've had in the past, in virtue of their membership in the grape category. Given your past experience, you assign that outcome a reasonably high expected positive value. (In real life, you probably do this implicitly rather than in any explicit way.) When you reason like this, it can be represented using computational modeling, where a higher-level categorization guides your reasoning about new lower-level cases (the new subtype of grapes) based on how you'd reason about the higher-level features that the new case shares with your previous experience.[33]

The grapes example brings out how, if you can identify which higher-order properties are relevant to the cognitive assessment of a new outcome, you can draw on your previous experience of these higher-order categorical properties in other, ostensibly quite different situations in order to construct a cognitive model of the new situation.

---

[33] This approach can be framed in terms of hierarchical Bayesian models (HBMs). A distinctive feature of HBMs is that they can be understood as flexible, responsive tools for learning, and that only a few experiences are needed for the human cognitive system to be able to recognize and exploit higher-order categorical similarities. You only need to try a few grapes to grasp what grapes of that kind are like, and the more grapes of different subtypes that you have, the more you can pinpoint and refine the higher order structure that they all share and that you should use in your inferences about grapes of a new subtype. Experience matters, and so you continuously update in response to new data. I'll come back to this point below when I discuss the long-term choice of raising a child. For relevant reading, see Tenenbaum, Kemp, Griffiths, and Goodman (2011).

In order to use this to partially model a transformative experience, think of the type of cognitive modeling you'd need to do as employing knowledge you have about higher-order structure to generate new knowledge about the transformative experience. You take the higher-order structure that you abstract from sets of past experiences and use it to map out higher-order features of possible future experiences, much like you might lay a sheet of rice paper over a picture to trace its outline and then use it to generate a new drawing with the same form, but with different colors, different media and in a different setting. The relevant higher-order experiential facts are what should remain the same across the modeling of the very different, lower or first-order experiences.

This fact about human cognition can be exploited in certain cases of epistemic transformation. Consider the way we reformulated the choice to try a durian from chapter 2. If you've never tasted a durian, you don't know what it will taste like, and people have very different reactions to it. However, you might reason as follows: I like the way grapes taste, and given that fact, I like the way fruit tastes. Since I like fruit, I should try a durian. Here, you are drawing on your experience of grapes, which is experience of something with the property of *being fruit*, and evaluating the novel outcome of tasting a durian under the assumption that this outcome, because it is an experience of tasting something with the same higher-order property, *being fruit*, will have an experientially similar character.

There is something about this procedure which is clearly right, and which connects to the importance of using the subjective perspective to assess future outcomes. We should draw on our previous experience to make inferences about future outcomes, and while the outcome might be epistemically transformative at the level of our experience of the first-order properties, for example, at the level of like *what it's like to taste durian*, it might not be epistemically transformative at higher levels. If this were the case for our fruit examples, we should be able to draw on our experience of higher-order properties such as *what it's like to taste fruit* in order to partially assess the subjective value of the outcome of tasting durian.

Of course, since the shared feature between the experience of tasting grapes and the experience of tasting durian is the higher-order feature of the experience of tasting fruit, the contribution of this experience to the model for the overall subjective value of tasting durian will only be partial: you won't know much about the details of the experience, just something about its general character.

One problem which the durian example brings out is that just knowing about this sort of general, higher-level structure, even if there is no higher-level epistemic transformation, might not help enough. This is because the higher-order structure or features of the outcomes may not contribute enough to the overall subjective value of the novel outcomes to matter. As we discussed in chapter 2, the response to the taste of durian varies widely, even amongst those who (usually) love fruit. In the durian case, it seems that the subjective intensity of the lower-order properties about the particular taste and smell properties of the durian sometimes swamps the contribution that its generically fruity features make to the experience.

This brings out how there might be many ways in which one's experience of higher-order features are not a useful guide to the subjective value of the novel outcome. Perhaps the experience of the higher-order structure is simply not the experience we notice when we assess the subjective value of the new experience. Perhaps we do notice it, but its value is swamped by the value of our experience of the new lower-order properties. Perhaps other higher-order properties of the novel experience are the properties that determine the subjective value of the novel experience, and so on. Only if we draw on the *right* experiences of higher-order features when assessing the novel experience, and those experiences of higher-order features *matter* to the subjective value of the novel experience, can we exploit this feature of cognition to make progress on modeling outcomes of transformative choices in a way that is subjectively useful.

The problem derives from the fact that, while we can use higher-order cognitive modeling to assess the higher-order subjective value of novel experiences, because the experience is epistemically transformative, we cannot know which, if any, of the experiences of higher-order features that have contributed to the subjective value of previous experiences will carry over to the values we assign to outcomes of the epistemically transformative experience. (At least, we cannot know on the basis of our personal experience alone, because we don't know what the new experience will be like.)

A different issue arises when the experience is transformative at higher levels, especially if it is transformative in a way that confounds prediction. The durian case is low-stakes, and so is not personally transformative. But individuals can experience preference change when they undergo experiences that are simultaneously epistemically and personally transformative. If the decision-maker's preference changes are epistemically inaccessible to her, then there is a second reason why she may not be able to determine which higher-order features she should rely upon when assessing subjective values of future possible outcomes: which higher-order features matter to her assessment may depend on how she responds to the experience.

These problems bring out how, if an individual cannot know what it is like to have the transformative experience, before she has the experience, she cannot know, from her experience alone, which higher-order similarities between her future experience and her previous experiences are the ones that matter.

But what she *can* do in this situation, given that, in principle, we think we should be able to use knowledge from previous experience to model novel experiences in cases involving transformative experience, is use empirical work from psychology and cognitive science to try to determine the right higher-order features to use when making top-down inferences about these novel subjective outcomes.

In other words, perhaps we can use empirical findings about first personal values and preference changes to help us determine which of our own higher-order features from which of our own experiences, if any, we should use when, as individuals, we cognitively model our different possible outcomes for our acts involving transformative experiences. We can then use empirical findings and Bayesian modeling techniques, not to eliminate the subjective, first personal perspective, but to guide our understanding of how to selectively draw on our previous experiences to construct and evaluate possible outcomes for our subjective futures.

How might this work? There are many models for inductive learning that explore how higher-order structure is applied to discover facts about new situations. One promising approach, as I've suggested, uses hierarchical Bayesian modeling[34] to find relevant abstract features drawn from our past experiences to probabilistically model our future ones. The Bayesian approach is especially useful for modeling how we can make strong inductive inferences from very sparse data and learn rapidly and flexibly. Such models for learning could be used in conjunction with data drawn from work on individuals who have had the relevant sorts of transformative experiences to help identify the higher-order structure needed for a successful forward mapping.[35] Employing cognitive models for inductive learning, where the right inductive constraint is empirically determined by finding the relevant structural similarity at the cognitive phenomenological level, could provide the first step towards constructing a new way to meet the normative rational standard for transformative decision-making.

The key is finding the right "overhypothesis": that is, finding the right higher-order structure to use to map forward to the phenomenologically new outcomes. This is related to the problem that has surfaced elsewhere when we wanted to use empirical information to

[34] Tenenbaum, Griffiths, and Kemp (2006).
[35] "The hierarchical Bayesian approach shows how knowledge can be simultaneously acquired at multiple levels of abstraction... Hierarchical Bayesian models (HBMs) include representations at multiple levels of abstraction, and show how knowledge can be acquired at levels quite remote from the data given by experience" (Kemp, Perfors, and Tenenbaum 2007, pp. 307–8).

guide us through our responses to transformative experiences, for example, when we wanted to use survey data to help us decide to have a child in chapter 3, and in this Afterword's sections on informed consent and the fundamental identity problem.[36]

The beauty of the work on hierarchical Bayesian modeling is that it shows how humans are actually able to *discover* or generate over-hypotheses from very few experiences and then go on to use these overhypotheses to manipulate and understand their environments. In other words, research in cognitive science on probabilistic models for cognition and learning shows how incredibly good humans are at determining the right hypothesis to use, once they have just a little bit of evidence.[37]

This means that, when assessing future experiences, because of the levels of structure involved, we may be able to discover the relevant overhypothesis (one drawn from a higher-order level) given a combination of some data, layers of increasingly abstract structure, our ability to learn inductively from sparse data, and the existence of phenomenal similarities between the right categories of experiences. Assumptions about hypotheses at even higher levels are still necessary, but the hope is that the relevant nth higher-order hypothesis could be discovered from a combination of first-order experiences, the right n+1st higher-order hypothesis, and induction.

For example: you might assume *I like to try new foods* as a hypothesis, and, by combining this with some first-order experiences at different restaurants, along with your experience of liking grapes of different types, discover that, in particular, that you don't especially like trying new food of just any type, for example, you don't really like trying

---

[36] "In Bayesian epistemology, *the problem of the priors* is this: How should we set our credences (or degrees of belief) in the absence of evidence? That is, how should we set our *prior* or *initial* credences, the credences with which we begin our credal life? David Lewis liked to call an agent at the beginning of her credal journey a *superbaby*" Pettigrew (2016). Knowledge of Lewis's "superbaby" phrase comes by way of testimony from Alan Hájek.

[37] Griffiths, Chater, Kemp, Perfors, and Tenenbaum (2010).

new fish-based dishes. What you really like about trying new foods is the experience of trying new *fruits*. You can then take *I like to try new kinds of fruit* as your overhypothesis, and use it to projectively model the outcome of trying a durian for the first time.

So the suggestion is that, at least for some types of cases, we could use higher-order cognitive phenomenological similarities to model and partly value new phenomenological outcomes, and in particular, use Bayesian learning techniques to discover which higher-order cognitive phenomenological similarities are the right ones to employ for this task. How might such a strategy help in our high-stakes cases of transformative experience?

Consider our congenitally blind saxophonist. Should he have retinal surgery, if the choice were available? Should he choose to become sighted? Part of the choice must certainly involve consideration of the question of whether the subjective value of gaining a new sensory capacity and discovering the new experiences it provides is higher than the value of keeping things on the phenomenally same track.

To assess the subjective value of the outcome of becoming sighted, the blind saxophone player would need to use higher-order structure to move cross-modally from a familiar sensory situation to a different, unfamiliar sensory situation. Even though the experience of being blind is very different from the experience of being sighted, some of the musician's previous experience might have the right sort of higher-order structure to allow him, from his own cognitive phenomenological perspective, to trace the experiential form and use it to model possible outcomes involving the experience of being sighted. If there is indeed any higher-order structure that would be shared by the musician's experiences before the retinal surgery and his possible experiences after the surgery, and if there is a way for him to identify and know that structure, he could use it as a partial guide for evaluating how his life could change.

The challenges here are significant. The first challenge involves the question of whether there *is* any relevant higher-order structure or form shared by the lived experience of blind adults and sighted adults that could give the saxophonist relevant knowledge about what it is like to see, such that he could evaluate possible outcomes of the decision to have a retinal transplant. Some of the values for these outcomes could depend, crucially, on the subjective value of what it would be like for him to see. Moreover, his ability to determine the expected value of choosing the surgery depends on his ability to determine how he'd value its possible outcomes given any relevant changes in his preferences. The problem is difficult, for it is unclear what sort of means we have to determine the candidate higher-order structure that he could use. What features of his previous experience could he draw on to make the needed assessments or to project his possible preferences?

Neuroscientific research suggests that the experience of being sighted is radically different from the experience of the blind, for blindness causes neural reorganization, and there are significant overall differences between the visual and occipital cortexes of blind and sighted individuals. And, intuitively, it might seem that the congenitally blind, at least those with little or no visual capacities, must differ from the sighted with respect to their concepts of vision or action terms like "to show" or "to run," as well as of color predicates like "is purple," given the differences in the character of their dominant sensory experiences. Many theorists, dating at least from Berkeley, have agreed.[38] The view might seem to be confirmed by detectable

---

[38] Berkeley (1948–57). Or, for example, see Adam Smith (1795): "Colour, the visible, bears no resemblance to solidity, the tangible object. A man born blind, or who has lost his Sight so early as to have no remembrance of visible objects, can form no idea or conception of colour. . . But though he might thus be able to name the different colours, which those different surfaces reflected, though he might thus have some imperfect notion of the remote causes of these Sensations, he could have no better idea of the Sensations themselves, than that other blind man, mentioned by Mr. Locke, had, who said that he imagined the Colour of Scarlet resembled the Sound of a Trumpet. A man born deaf may, in the same manner, be taught to speak articulately. He is taught how to shape and dispose of his organs, so as to pronounce each letter, syllable, and word. But still, though he may have some imperfect idea of the remote causes of the Sounds which he himself utters, of the remote causes of the Sensations which he himself excites in other people; he can have none of those Sounds or Sensations themselves."

differences in neural activity between blind and sighted individuals when they are performing similar linguistic tasks.[39]

But new research (Bedny and Saxe (2012)) suggests that the sensory visual experiences of normally sighted adults and the sensory experiences of the blind, including the congenitally blind, while deeply different at the level of first-order experience, are nevertheless similarly structured at a higher cognitive level. In particular, seemingly vision-based concepts like "to run" had by congenitally blind adults seem to share higher-order conceptual structure with the concepts had by sighted individuals. The researchers conclude that:

> While the sensory experience of blind and sighted people is drastically different, behavioral and neuroimaging data show that conceptual representations of these two groups are strikingly similar. These similarities hold for conceptual categories that, in our view, are among the best candidates to show effects of blindness. Conceptual representations used to understand concrete words, categorize objects and actions, and think about the perceptual states of other people are not images of sensory experiences. Humans have a rich repertoire of abstract representations that capture the higher-order structure of their environment in terms of events, objects, agents, and their mental states.[40]

This research suggests that there may indeed be some sort of higher-order structure available for a cross-modal application of blind experience to sighted experience. Obviously, questions abound, given the empirical underdetermination of the facts. What exactly is the form of the structure shared by the blind and the sighted? Is it structure that could be exploited, in much the same way as we exploited higher-order structure about trying new foods to discover the value of trying new fruit? Is there a relevant nth-order phenomenal similarity connected to shared conceptual structure that is somehow experienced in a way that could give the blind the ability to assign partial subjective values to what it is like to see?

---

[39] Bedny and Saxe (2012).
[40] Bedny and Saxe (2012, p. 74).

If the relevant structure exists and can be discovered, the blind saxophonist could, in principle, use this research to locate and draw on his relevantly similar previous experiences to identify the right abstract structure for the assessment of possible future outcomes and to model possible changes in preferences. Once the right inductive guidelines were established, he could draw on his previous experience of outcomes with this higher-order structure to construct partial models of novel visual experiential outcomes and assign them partial subjective values based on what he knows outcomes with the right abstract structure would be like. To the extent that the blind saxophonist can evaluate the subjective values of having new sensory modalities, perhaps he could predict relevant preference changes and map forward to outcomes involving what it would be like for him to experience a new sense modality while experiencing an altered auditory capacity. This would give him an empirically supported method to use when trying to assign values and make big decisions about radically new experiences.

Obviously, even if the blind saxophonist can model *something* that will give him information about the subjective value of the new sense modality of vision, the subjective value of *what it is like to see*, in its full first-order manifestations, will still be inaccessible to him. As a result, even with the new strategy in place, we still come back to the fact that the radically new experience involved in transformative choice is epistemically and personally transformative. What it is like to see will have a complex effect on the saxophonist, since in addition to changing the way he organizes and lives his life, and changing his relationships with his family and friends, it will change his auditory and tactile experiences, which are likely to change many of his central lived experiences, including his experience of playing the saxophone. Presumably, these knock-on effects will have a major impact on his preferences and so on the expected value, for him, of becoming a sighted individual. In the case of the blind saxophonist, then, to have a successful partial model that will be of any significant use, he must find structure that supports an assessment of what it is like to see that is deep enough to give him the knowledge he needs in order to determine what his new preferences will be as the result of becoming sighted.

So the structure he uses will have to be informative enough to tell him enough about what it is like to experience seeing, so that he can successfully model his new preferences (which would form as the result of becoming sighted) when he evaluates the values of the outcomes from the choice to have retinal surgery. Or the structure must be complex enough to build this change of preferences in without his explicit knowledge of them, so that when he models his outcomes, the structure guides him to values for outcomes that reflect both his new knowledge of what it is like to see plus his new preferences as a sighted individual. This means that we need an extensive and far-reaching, highly developed abstract structure, one sensitive to facts about deep cognitive structure that might be constant across sensory modalities as well as to facts about deep cognitive structure that might be constant across major personal changes.

In addition, we face the computational limits of the experiencer: that is, while we have impressive capacities to model future outcomes, the abstract nature of the similarities we must rely on to model radically new outcomes may pose computational hurdles when we try to model these cognitively complex outcomes. In particular, some particularly important but causally downstream outcomes might be caused by the first-order nature of what it is like to see, and so might be especially hard to model. In other words, because what it is like to see will have a complex causal effect on the saxophonist, with many causal implications, it may be computationally intractable for him to model the relevant outcomes with only abstract structure to guide him. Moreover, we may not be able to effectively predict or evaluate changes in preferences that would occur solely because of the first-order qualitative character of what it is like for him to see. And so, in high-stakes cases like this, where the intensity and kind of the transformative experience changes one's personal preferences, there are still no obvious solutions. This does not mean that using higher-order structure doesn't help us with transformative choices; it means that such help may only be partial. But partial help is better than no help at all.

The case of the blind saxophonist brings out just how challenging it would be to uncover the right sort of higher-order structure to use in our inferences, but the fascinating work by Bedny and Saxe (2012) also makes the strategy seem at least potentially workable. If it did work, we'd have an example of how we can use models designed for partial ignorance of subjective values when making a transformative choice—even though we don't know what the first personal "on-the-ground" experience would be like—as long as we know enough about the abstract structure of that experience to start to predict and assign values.

The value of discovering the relevant higher-order structure is not that such structure can tell us everything about what it is like to have a transformative experience, but that it gives us a way to make an empirically supported, rational *start* on the decision problem. It points us in a direction we might take to develop a rough and approximate way of making a rational transformative choice involving a radically new discovery about the character of an experience.[41] It highlights a way that cognitive science, by discovering information about the relevant higher-order hypotheses, could be of use to those contemplating transformative choices.

My discussion in this section suggests a blueprint for further empirical work. But in the absence of such empirical work, for those of us who want to decide right now, for example, whether to have a child, how are we to proceed? How can we rationally approach transformative decisions before the empirical work pointing to how to determine and employ the right overhypothesis has been done? As I suggested in chapter 4, reformulating the decision in terms of revelation seems like the best option. One way to frame the deliberation is predicated on our ignorance of the values of the outcomes.

---

[41] There are connections here to using hierarchical Bayesian models to represent features of Kuhnian paradigm shifts in contexts of scientific discovery and revolution. See Henderson, Goodman, Tenenbaum, and Woodward (2010).

If you are a Bayesian, perhaps you could embrace a hierarchical Bayesian approach to transformative choices based on revelation. The goal would be to generate a highly abstract overhypothesis about the value of revelation that you could employ when making personal decisions. *If* you have the right sort of evidence about the safety level of your environment (that's a big *if*), the place to start when making a transformative choice might involve the generation and assessment of very general overhypotheses, such as the hypothesis that *I like transformative experiences*, or the hypothesis that *I dislike transformative experiences*. You might be able to assess these hypotheses by consulting your previous experience of particular transformative experiences (trying radically new activities, going to college, and so on) together with an assessment of the safety and the stability of your local environment to determine which hypothesis is the right one to employ. In this way, you might be able to draw from your previous experience to partly guide your transformative choices on the basis of the desirability of revelation.

## Unawareness

Another effective strategy for transformative decision-making might be to look to alternative models for rational decision-making under severe epistemic constraints. Work on decision-making under conditions of extreme ignorance, described as situations where agents make decisions where they are unaware of the outcomes,[42] including situations where they do not know the values of possible outcomes of their decision, may be of help here.[43]

Imagine a game between a talented chess player and a mediocre one, where it is the mediocre chess player's turn to move. The mediocre player knows there are moves he can make that will have desirable

---

[42] I am particularly indebted to Joe Halpern and John Quiggin for discussion.
[43] Heifetz, Meier, and Schipper (2006); Halpern and Rêgo (2009); Halpern and Rêgo (2013); and Quiggin and Grant (2013).

and undesirable outcomes, but he is unable to visualize the game more than one or two moves ahead, and he has not memorized any appropriate tactics he could use to predict outcomes resulting from particular moves. So, he knows there are moves he could make, and these moves will result in particular outcomes of arrangements of pieces on the chess board, say, five or ten moves later, but he doesn't know what these outcomes are. He cannot, by himself, map out the game tree more than one or two steps ahead, and he has no strategy or tactical plan that he can use to determine or predict the outcomes for him, so he is unable to know the outcomes of the different moves he is choosing between.

So, the mediocre chess player knows there will be outcomes a few steps down the tree that will result from his moves, but he doesn't know what those outcomes are. Thus, he cannot work out the different possible paths from his next move to those outcomes, and he cannot proceed by calculating the expected value of his next move in the usual way. In this situation, how should he make his move? That is, how should he move in order to maximize his chance of winning, given the extreme computational constraints he faces? Is there nothing for him to do but make a random guess?

No. Even if he can't work out the consequences of his acts, he has other facts at his disposal, such as what he knows in general about the merits of various board positions, whether he wants to play a defensive game or take a more aggressive approach, and the worth of various chess pieces (he knows the difference, say, between the usefulness of having a Queen versus the usefulness of having a Rook). He can engage in positional, rather than tactical, play.

What the literature on decision-making with unawareness discusses is how an agent in a situation like that of the mediocre chess player can maximize the rationality of his moves using other types of information he has at his disposal.[44] So, for example, in the chess

---

[44] "While an agent cannot make decisions based on facts that he is unaware of, it is clear that awareness of unawareness can have a significant impact in decision making" (Halpern and Rêgo 2009).

game, the mediocre player can act rationally if he acts with the right understanding of how he is not aware of various outcomes. That is, he can act rationally if he acts with the knowledge that there are outcomes that he is "unaware" of in the relevant sense, making his choice of move in a way that is constrained by this knowledge, while also being guided by any justified strategic principles and general evidence he has at his disposal.

We can apply this approach to the problem of transformative decision-making. Compare the choice the mediocre chess player must take to the choice you are to make between the ability to taste and having an entirely new sensory ability. When approaching the decision of whether to trade in your sense of taste, the main thing to recognize is that you cannot make this decision based on what it is like to have the new sensory ability in place of the old. You know that possible outcomes exist where your ability to taste is replaced by your new sensory capacity, but because you don't know what it would be like to experience these outcomes, you cannot simulate them from your first personal perspective. Since you cannot know these outcomes, you cannot value them, nor (let us assume) can you assign probabilities to states that lead to them, nor can you eliminate particular probability assignments from your set of possibilities. Thus, you cannot determine the expected values of your alternatives.

If you could know, through empirical work, which of the higher-order experiential features of the sensory abilities you already have are relevantly similar to the new sense, you might be able to exploit this information to help you make your choice. But we are also assuming that you are the first person to get the new microchip, and so there is no empirical evidence like this to draw on.[45]

---

[45] You might still want to use the models for unawareness if you had empirical information from cognitive science about common higher-order structure, since even with that information you'd only be able to partially model outcomes. The empirical information, in addition to guiding the construction of cognitive models of outcomes, could provide support for using certain general principles.

In such a situation, work on unawareness may give us a way to develop a decision model. Like the mediocre chess player, you know there exist outcomes you are unaware of, and so you act accordingly, constraining your decision by what you know, in general terms, about sensory abilities. For example, presumably, the new sense ability will involve some special capacity to detect new secondary qualities of the world. It might enhance or detract from other sensory capacities like smell or sight. While you cannot imagine or entertain scenarios that can tell you what it would be like for you to have this new sensory ability, you can use your general knowledge of what sense capacities are like to guide your decision.

In this sort of epistemically constrained context of discovery, facts about, broadly speaking, the safety and stability of your environment become especially relevant. If you have inductive or other evidence that you are in an unstable or unsafe environment, you should follow a precautionary principle when making a decision under unawareness, which suggests that you prefer acts that lead to known values and preferences.[46] If you have evidence that you are in a stable and safe environment, or evidence that mistakes can be easily corrected, you should follow an exploratory principle, which suggests that you prefer acts that can lead to the discovery of new, previously unknown values and preferences.[47]

Once we see what we'd need to do to reformulate and constrain the decision in order to make it rational, however, the epistemic poverty of our situation is laid bare. The proposal is that a decision is to be guided only by the broad contours and constraints of the decision space, that is, it is to proceed with almost no information or awareness of the qualitative nature of the particular unknown outcomes.

Considering this in the context of your decision about sensory abilities, what would life be like without the taste of wine, ripe peaches, or

[46] Grant and Quiggin (2013).

[47] Given that learning new information can have significant value for causally downstream decisions, having a new experience can be of high value.

French cheese, yet with a radically new sensory approach to the world? Who knows? You cannot make your decision on the basis of knowing what your life with the different abilities would be like. All you can use to make your choice are some very general, high-level facts about how you'd lose one kind of ability to experience the world and gain another, while the sensory abilities you kept might be altered in some way, in conjunction with an exploratory principle that supports revelation or a precautionary principle that constrains revelation.

This takes us, then, back to the position developed at the end of chapter 4, where decisions are framed, not in terms of comparisons of the details of different ways of experiencing the world, but in terms of the value and the cost of revelation. When you make a transformative decision, what you assess is the value of revelation, that is, you choose between the alternatives of discovering what it is like to have the new preferences and experiences involved in the transformative change, or keeping the life that you know, and you may only be able to make this assessment by relying on very general, and very abstract, facts.

## Conclusion: Revelation

There are two kinds of issues raised by transformative experiences. First, we can't, despite the way the story is often told, approach transformative decisions by stepping back and evaluating our different subjective possibilities, imaginatively modeling outcomes and reflecting on the expected subjective values of our actions. In a situation of transformative choice, if we choose to have the transformative experience, we simply don't know enough about what our lived experience will be like afterwards. We lack the ability to assign subjective values to the outcomes of the act and to determine how our preferences might evolve. This has philosophical and practical implications for the way we live our lives, for as individuals who want to live rational, authentic lives, we are forced to confront the existential implications of our epistemic limitations.

Second, we need to develop new decision-theoretic models if we want to use normative decision theory as a guide for rational transformative choice, and this opens up new directions for research.

So we need to think differently about how we plan our futures, and about how, as rational decision-makers, we configure our decisions. As I've argued, we should draw on empirical findings when the right sorts of findings are available, and in this Afterword, I've discussed some promising theoretical and empirical ways to make inroads on modeling transformative choices. But, crucially, in addition to managing the decision-theoretic worries using more sophisticated modeling techniques, resolving the problems raised by transformative experience also involves valuing experience for its own sake, that is, for the revelation it brings.

Here, we connect back to the importance of subjective values, and how such valuing is distinct from merely valuing happiness or pleasure and pain. When we choose to have a transformative experience, we choose to discover its intrinsic experiential nature, whether that discovery involves joy, fear, peacefulness, happiness, fulfillment, sadness, anxiety, suffering, or pleasure, or some complex mixture thereof. If we choose to have the transformative experience, we also choose to create and discover new preferences, that is, to experience the way our preferences will evolve, and often, in the process, to create and discover a new self. On the other hand, if we reject revelation, we choose the status quo, affirming our current life and lived experience. A life lived rationally and authentically, then, as each big decision is encountered, involves deciding whether or how to make a discovery about who you will become. If revelation comes from experience, independently of the (first-order) pleasure or pain of the experience, there can be value in discovering how one's preferences and lived experience develop, simply for what such experience teaches. One of the most important games of life, then, is the game of Revelation, a game played for the sake of play itself.

# BIBLIOGRAPHY

Agar, Nick (2010) *Humanity's End: Why We Should Reject Radical Enhancement.* Cambridge, MA: MIT Bradford Press.

Appiah, Kwame Anthony (2008) *Experiments in Ethics.* Cambridge, MA: Harvard University Press.

Aristotle (1923) *Metaphysics.* Trans. W. D. Ross. London: Methuen and Co.

Barnes, Elizabeth (2016) *The Minority Body.* Oxford: Oxford University Press.

Battaglia P., Hamrick J., and Tenenbaum J., (2013) "Simulation as an engine of physical scene understanding," *Proceedings of the National Academy of Sciences,* 110 (45): 18327–32.

Bayne, Tim and Montague, Michelle (eds) (2011) *Cognitive Phenomenology.* Oxford: Oxford University Press.

Becker, Gary S. (1998) *Accounting for Tastes.* Cambridge, MA: Harvard University Press.

Becker, Howard S., Geer, Blanche, Hughes, Everett C., and Strauss, Anselm (1961) *Boys in White: Student Culture in Medical School.* Chicago: University of Chicago Press.

Bedny M., and Saxe, R. (2012) "Insights into the origins of knowledge from the cognitive neuroscience of blindness," *Cognitive Neuropsychology,* 29 (1–2): 56–84.

Berkeley, G. (1948–57) "An essay towards a new theory of vision," in *Works* 1: 171–239, *The Works of George Berkeley, Bishop of Cloyne,* ed. A. A. Luce and T. E. Jessop. London: Thomas Nelson and Sons.

Blankmeyer Burke, Teresa (2014) "Armchairs and stares: On the privation of deafness," in *Deaf Gain: Re-imagining Human Diversity,* ed. H. Dirksen, L. Bauman, and J. Murray. Minnesota: University of Minnesota Press.

Brase, Gary L. and Brase, Sandra L. (2012) "Emotional regulation of fertility decision making: What is the nature and structure of 'baby fever'?" *Emotion* 12 (5): 1141–54.

Brown, Vincent (2003) "Spiritual terror and sacred authority in Jamaican slave society," *Slavery and Abolition: A Journal of Slave and Post-Slave Studies,* 24 (1): 24–53.

Buchak, Lara (2014) *Risk and Rationality.* Oxford: Oxford University Press.

Buchak, Lara (2016) "Decision theory," in *Oxford Handbook of Probability and Philosophy,* ed. Christopher Hitchcock and Alan Hájek. Oxford: Oxford University Press.

Campbell, John (1993) "A Simple View of Colour," in *Reality: Representation and Projection*, ed. John J. Haldane and C. Wright. Oxford: Oxford University Press, 257–68.

Carel, Havi (2014a) "Ill, but well: a phenomenology of wellbeing in chronic illness," in *Disability and the Good Life*, ed. J. Bickenbach, F. Felder, and B. Schmitz. Cambridge: Cambridge University Press, 243–70.

Carel, Havi (2014b) *Phenomenology of Illness*. Oxford: Oxford University Press.

Carr, Jennifer (n.d.) "Epistemic Utility Theory and the Aim of Belief," unpublished MS.

Chang, Ruth (ed.) (1997) "Introduction," in *Incommensurability, Incomparability and Practical Reason*, Cambridge, MA: Harvard University Press.

Chang, Ruth (2012) "Are hard choices cases of incomparability?" *Philosophical Issues*, 22 (1): 106–26.

Colyvan, Mark (2006) "No expectations," *Mind*, 115: 695–702.

Conrad, Joseph (1990) *Heart of Darkness* (unabridged). New York: Dover Publications.

Cowan, Philip A., and Cowan, Carolyn Pape (1995) "How working with couples fosters children's development: From prevention science to public policy," in *Strengthening Couple Relationships for Optimal Child Development: Lessons from Research and Intervention*, ed. M. Schulz, M. Pruett, P. Kerig, and R. Parke. Washington, DC: American Psychological Association, 211–28.

Easwaran, Kenny (2008) "Strong and weak expectations," *Mind*, 117: 633–41.

Edin, Kathryn, and Kefalas, Maria J. (2007) *Promises I Can Keep: Why Poor Women Put Motherhood Before Marriage*. Berkeley: University of California Press.

Elga, Adam (2010) "Subjective probabilities should be sharp," *Philosophers' Imprint*, 10 (5): 1–11.

Ellenberg, Jordan (2013). Available online at: <http://quomodocumque.word-press.com/2013/03/12/what-is-it-like-to-be-a-vampire-andor-parent> accessed September 22, 2014.

Elster, Jon (1979) *Ulysses and the Sirens: Studies in Rationality and Irrationality*. Cambridge: Cambridge University Press.

Elster, Jon (1997) "More than enough," review of *Accounting for Tastes*, *University of Chicago Law Review*, 64: 749–64.

Evenson, Ranae, and Simon, Robin (2005) "Clarifying the relationship between parenthood and depression," *Journal of Health and Social Behavior*, 46 (4): 341–58.

Fantl, Jeremy, and McGrath, Matthew (2002) "Evidence, pragmatics, and justification," *The Philosophical Review*, 111 (1): 67–94.

Fine, Terrence (2008) "Evaluating the Pasadena, Altadena, and St. Petersburg gambles," *Mind*, 117: 613–32.

Flanagan, Owen (1991) *Varieties of Moral Personality*. Cambridge, MA: Harvard University Press.

Fussell, P. (1989) *Wartime: Understanding and Behavior in the Second World War*. New York: Oxford University Press.

*The Guardian* (2014) "Durian, the world's smelliest fruit, goes on sale in Britain," February 3. Available at: <http://www.theguardian.com/lifeandstyle/wordofmouth/2014/feb/03/durian-worlds-smelliest-fruit-sale-britain> accessed April 23, 2014.

Gibbons, John (2010) "Things that make things reasonable," *PPR*, LXXXI (2): 335–61.

Gilbert, D. (2007) *Stumbling on Happiness*. New York: Vintage.

Godfrey Smith, Peter (2013) "On being an octopus: Diving deep in search of the human mind," *Boston Review*, June 3.

Goff, Philip (2011) "A posteriori physicalists get our phenomenal concepts wrong," *Australasian Journal of Philosophy* 89: 191–209.

Grant, S., and Quiggin, J. (2013) "Bounded awareness, heuristics and the precautionary principle," *Journal of Economic Behavior and Organization*, 93: 17–31.

Griffiths, T. L., Chater, N., Kemp, C., Perfors, A., and Tenenbaum, J. B. (2010) "Probabilistic models of cognition: Exploring representations and inductive biases," *Trends in Cognitive Sciences*, 14 (8): 357–64.

Haidt, J. (2006) *The Happiness Hypothesis*. New York: Basic Books.

Hájek, Alan (2007) "The reference class problem is your problem too," *Synthese*, 156: 185–15.

Hájek, Alan, and Nover, Harris (2004) "Vexing expectations," *Mind*, 113: 237–49.

Hájek, Alan, and Nover, Harris (2006) "Perplexing expectations," *Mind*, 115: 703–20.

Hájek, Alan, and Nover, Harris (2008) "Complex expectations," *Mind*, 117: 643–64.

Halpern, J., and Rêgo, L. (2009) "Reasoning about knowledge of unawareness," *Games and Economic Behavior*, 67 (2): 503–25.

Halpern, J., and Rêgo, L. (2013) "Reasoning about knowledge of unawareness revisited," *Mathematical Social Sciences*, 65 (2): 73–84.

Harman, Elizabeth (2009) "'I'll be glad I did it': Reasoning and the significance of future desires," *Philosophical Perspectives*, 23: 177–99.

Hawthorne, J., and Stanley, J. (2008) "Knowledge and action," *The Journal of Philosophy*, CV (10): 571–90.

Haybron, Daniel M. (2007) "Do we know how happy we are? On some limits of affective introspection and recall," *Noûs*, 41 (3): 394–428.

Healy, Kieran (2006) *Last Best Gifts*. Chicago: University of Chicago Press.

Heckman, James J., Lopes, Hedibert F., and Piatek, Rémi (2014) "Treatment effects: A Bayesian perspective," *Econometric Reviews*, Special Issue in Honor of Arnold Zellner (33): 36–67.

Hedden, Brian (2015) "Time-slice rationality," *Mind* 124 (494): 449–491.

Heifetz, A., Meier, M., and Schipper, B. (2006), "Interactive unawareness," *Journal of Economic Theory*, 130 (1): 78–94.

Henderson, L., Goodman, N. D., Tenenbaum, J. B., and Woodward, J. F. (2010) "The structure and dynamics of scientific theories: A hierarchical Bayesian perspective," *Philosophy of Science*, 77 (2): 172–200.

Horgan, T. and Tienson, J. (2002) "The intentionality of phenomenology and the phenomenology of intentionality," in *Philosophy of Mind: Classical and Contemporary Readings*, ed. D. Chalmers. Oxford: Oxford University Press, 520–32.

Howard Griffin, John (1961) *Black Like Me*. Boston: Houghton Mifflin.

Hyman, John (1999) "How knowledge works", *The Philosophical Quarterly*, 49 (197): 433–51.

Ismael, Jenann (forthcoming) "Passage, flow and the logic of temporal perspectives," in *The Nature of Time, The Time of Nature*, ed. Christophe Bouton and Philippe Hunemann. Chicago: University of Chicago Press.

Jackson, Frank (1982) "Epiphenomenal qualia," *Philosophical Quarterly*, 32: 127–36.

Johnston, Mark (1992) "How to speak of the colours," *Philosophical Studies*, 68: 221–63.

Joyce, James (2010) "In defense of imprecise probabilities in decision-making and inference," *Philosophical Perspectives*, 24 (1): 281–323.

Kahneman, D. (2013) *Thinking, Fast and Slow*. New York: Farrar, Straus and Giroux.

Kahneman, Daniel, and Kreuger, Alan (2006) "Developments in the measurement of subjective well-being," *Journal of Economic Perspectives*, 20 (1): 3–24.

Kahneman, Daniel, Krueger, Alan, Schkade, David, Schwarz, Norbert, and Stone, Arthur (2004) "A survey method for characterizing daily life experience: The day reconstruction method," *Science*, 306 (5702): 1776–80.

Keegan, J. (1976) *The Face of Battle*. London: Jonathan Cape.

Kemp, C., Perfors, A., and Tenenbaum, J. B. (2007) "Learning overhypotheses with hierarchical Bayesian models," *Developmental Science*, 10 (3): 307–21.

Kolodny, Niko (2003) "Love as valuing a relationship," *Philosophical Review*, 1122: 135–89.

Kukla, Rebecca (2005) "Conscientious autonomy: What patients do vs. what is done to them," *Hastings Center Report*, 35 (2): 34–44.

Levy, Neil (2002) "Reconsidering cochlear implants: The lessons of Martha's Vineyard," *Bioethics*, 16 (2): 134–53.

Levy, Neil (2014) "Forced to be free? Increasing patient autonomy by constraining it," *Journal of Medical Ethics*. doi: 10.1136/medethics-2011-100207

Lewis, David (1988) "What experience teaches," *Proceedings of the Russellian Society*, University of Sydney, 13: 29–57.

Lewis, David (1989) "Dispositional theories of value," *Proceedings of the Aristotelian Society*, Supplementary Volume, 63: 113–37.

Lewis, David (1997) "Finkish dispositions," *Philosophical Quarterly*, 47 (187): 143–58.

Littlejohn, Clayton (2012) *Justification and the Truth-Connection*. Cambridge: Cambridge University Press.

McClanahan, Sara, and Julia Adams (1989) "The effects of children on adults' psychological wellbeing," *Social Forces*, 68 (1): 124–46.

Milne, A. A. (1926) *Winnie the Pooh*. London: Methuen.

Moran, Richard (2001) *Authority and Estrangement: An Essay on Self-knowledge*. Princeton: Princeton University Press.

Moss, Sarah (2015) "Credal dilemmas", Nous. vol. 49, no. 4 (2015): 665–83.

Nagel, Thomas (1974) "What is it like to be a bat?" *Philosophical Review*, 83: 435–50. Oxford: Oxford University Press.

Nagel, Thomas (1989) *The View From Nowhere*. Oxford: Oxford University Press.

Nelson, S. K., Kushlev, K., English,T., Dunn, E. W., and Lyubomirsky, S. (2013) "In defense of parenthood: Children are associated with more joy than misery," *Psychological Science*, 24 (1): 3–10.

*New York Daily News* (2013) "World's stinkiest fruit is turned into wine" July. Available online at: <http://www.nydailynews.com/life-style/eats/world-stinkiest-fruit-turned-wine-article-1.1411504> accessed April 23, 2014.

NIDCD (2014). "National Institute on Deafness and Other Communication Disorders: Cochlear Implants." Available online at: <http://www.nidcd.nih.gov/health/hearing/pages/coch.aspx> accessed September 22, 2014.

Nomaguchi, Kei, and Milkie, Melissa (2003) "Costs and rewards of children: The effects of becoming a parent on adults' lives," *Journal of Marriage and the Family*, 65 (2): 356–74.

Ouellette, Alicia (2011) "Hearing the deaf: Cochlear implants, the deaf community, and bioethical analysis," *Valparaiso University Law Review*, 45: 1247–63.

Parfit, Derek (1984) *Reasons and Persons*. Oxford: Oxford University Press.

Paul, L. A. (1997) "The Worm at the Root of the Passions: Poetry and sympathy in Mill's utilitarianism," *Utilitas*, 10: 83–104.

Paul, L. A. (n.d.) "Transformative religious belief," unpublished MS.

Paul, L.A. (2015a) "What you can't expect when you're expecting," *Res Philosophica*, Vol. 92, No. 2, April 2015, pp. 149–170.

Paul, L.A. (2015b)."Transformative Choice: Discussion and Replies", *Res Philosophica*, Vol. 92, No. 2, pp. 473–545.

Pettigrew, Richard (2016) "Accuracy, Risk, and the Principle of Indifference" *Philosophy and Phenomenological Research* 92(1):35–59.

Quiggin, J., and Grant, S. (2013) "Inductive reasoning about unawareness," *Economic Theory*, 54: 717–55.

Raz, Joseph (1988) *The Morality of Freedom*. Oxford: Oxford University Press.

Rothman, Joshua (2013) "The impossible decision," *New Yorker*, 23 April. Available at: <http://www.newyorker.com/online/blogs/books/2013/04/graduate-school-advice-impossible-decision.html> accessed 24 April 2014.

Rothman, Adam (2014) "The horrors '12 Years a Slave' couldn't tell," Al Jazeera January 18.

Sacks, Oliver (1991) *Seeing Voices: A Journey into the World of the Deaf*. London: Picador.

Savulescu, Julian, and Kahane, Guy (2009) "The moral obligation to create children with the best chance of the best life," *Bioethics*, 23 (5): 274–90.

Siegel, Susanna (2012) *The Contents of Visual Experience*. Oxford: Oxford University Press.

Simon, Robin (2008) "Life's greatest joy? The negative emotional effects of children on adults," *Contexts*, 7: 40–5.

Smith, Adam (1795) "Of the external senses," in *Glasgow Edition of the Works and Correspondence*, iii: *Essays on Philosophical Subjects*.

Solomon, Andrew (2013) *Far from the Tree: Parents, Children and the Search for Identity*. New York: Scribner.

Spriggs, M. (2002) "Lesbian couple create a child who is deaf like them," *Journal of Medical Ethics*, 28: 283.

*Talk of the Nation* (2006) Peter Artinian, interviewed by Neil Conan on (NPR, October 12 [radio interview].

Tenenbaum, J. B., Griffiths, T. L., and Kemp, C. (2006) "Theory-based Bayesian models of inductive learning and reasoning," *Trends in Cognitive Sciences*, 10 (7): 309–18.

Tenenbaum, J. B., Kemp, C., Griffiths, T. L., and Goodman, N. D. (2011) "How to grow a mind: Statistics, structure and abstraction," *Science*, 331 (6022): 1279–85.

Ullmann-Margalit, Edna (2006) "Big decisions: Opting, converting, drifting," *Royal Institute of Philosophy Supplements*, 81 (58): 157–72.

Ullmann-Margalit, Edna, and Morgenbesser, Sidney (1977) "Picking and choosing," *Social Research*, 44 (4, Winter): 757–89.

Unger, Peter (1975) *Ignorance: A Case for Skepticism*. Oxford: Clarendon Press.

van Fraassen, Bas (1984) "Belief and the will," *Journal of Philosophy*, 81 (5): 235–56.

Wallace, R. Jay (2013) *The View from Here: On Affirmation, Attachment and the Limits of Regret*. New York: Oxford University Press.

Weirich, Paul (2004) *Realistic Decision Theory: Rules for Nonideal Agents in Nonideal Circumstances*. Oxford: Oxford University Press.

Wilentz, C. J. (1988) "In the matter of Baby M," 537 A.2d 1227 (NJ 1988).

Wilson, Tim (2011) *Redirect: The Surprising New Science of Psychological Change*. New York: Little, Brown.

White, Roger (2010) "Evidential symmetry and mushy credences," in *Oxford Studies in Epistemology*, iii, ed. T. Szabo Gendler and J. Hawthorne. Oxford: Oxford University Press, 161–86.

Wolf, Susan (1982) "Moral saints," *Journal of Philosophy*, 79 (8): 419–39.

Zelizer, Viviana (1985) *Pricing the Priceless Child: The Changing Social Value of Children*. Princeton: Basic Books.

# GENERAL INDEX

# NAME INDEX

Barnes, Elizabeth. 56 n. 4
Becker, Gary S. 99 n. 53, 140 n. 18
Bedny M., and Saxe, R. 70 n. 20, 169, 172
Buchak, Lara 22 n. 25, 30 n. 37

Campbell, John 13 n. 17, 92 n. 51
Chang, Ruth 12 n. 15, 34 n. 43, 102 n. 55
Conrad, Joseph 123

Edin, Kathryn, and Kefalas, Maria J. 72 n.
 26, 78, 81 n. 41, 82 n. 42
Elster, Jon 91 n. 50, 140 n. 18

Gilbert, D. 20 n. 23, 21 n. 24, 77 n. 30, 79
 n. 34, 89 n. 47, 125 n. 1
Griffiths, T.L., Chater, N., Kemp, C.,
 Perfors, A., and Tenenbaum,
 J.B. 166 n. 37

Hájek, Alan, and Nover, Harris 33,
 142–143
Halpern, J., and Rêgo, L 173 n. 43, 174
 n. 44
Halpern J. 174
Harman Elizabeth 57 n. 6, 81 n. 41, 89
Healy, Kieran 140 n. 16
Heckman James J. 133 n. 10

Ismael, Jenann 105 n. 2, 106 n. 3

Jackson, Frank 8–9, 14 n. 18
Johnston, Mark 13 n. 17, 92 n. 51

Kahneman, D. 20 n. 23, 21 n. 24, 86 n. 45,
 89 n. 47, 125 n. 1

Keegan, J. 53 n. 2, 54 n. 3

Levy, Neil 61 n. 12, 67 n. 18, 139 n. 15
Lewis, David 10, 11 n. 13, 12, 92 n. 51,
 149 n. 23, 166 n. 36

Moran, Richard 130
Moss, Sarah 91 n. 49, 150 n. 26, 151 n. 27,
 157 n. 30

Nagel, Thomas 5–6, 11 n. 12

Ouellette, Alicia 65 n. 16

Parfit Derek 120 n. 10
Pettigrew, Richard 166 n. 36

Quiggin, John 176 n. 46

Raz, Joseph 34 n. 43, 103 n. 56

Sartre, Jean Paul 112, 122, 130

Tenenbaum, Josh 79 n. 24, 159 n. 32, 161
 n. 33, 165 n. 34, 165 n. 35, 166 n.
 37, 172 n. 41

Ullmann-Margalit, Edna 16 n. 20, 34
 n. 43

Van Fraassen, Bas 150

Wallace, R. Jay 77 n. 31, 96 n. 52
Weirich, Paul 20 n. 22, 22 n. 26, 30 n. 38,
 32 n. 40

The manufacturer's authorised representative in the EU for product
safety is Oxford University Press España S.A. of El Parque Empresarial
San Fernando de Henares, Avenida de Castilla, 2 - 28830 Madrid
(www.oup.es/en or product.safety@oup.com). OUP España S.A. also acts
as importer into Spain of products made by the manufacturer.
Printed and bound by CPI Group (UK) Ltd, Croydon, CR0 4YY

22/01/2025
01824116-0002